Introducing Islamic Financial Transactions

By Safaruk Z. Chowdhury

Introducing Islamic Financial Transactions

by
Safaruk Z. Chowdhury

AD-DUHA 2013

First edition 2007
Second Edition 2008
Updated Edition 2010

An educational publication from Ad-Duha London
Third Floor, 42 Fieldgate Street
London E1 1ES
E: info@duha.org.uk
W: www.duha.org.uk
T: 07891 421 925

First unpublished edition 2007

Title : Introducing Islamic Financial Transactions

By : S. Z. Chowdhury

Published : 2013

Book available in:

- Europe
- USA
- United Kingdom

www.amazon.co.uk

Ad-Duha London
Third Floor, 42 Fieldgate Street
M: 07891 421 925
E: info@duha.org.uk
W: www.duha.org.uk

Transliteration System

Arabic Letter	Transliteration
ء	’
ب	b
ت	t
ث	th
ج	j
ح	ḥ
خ	kh
د	d
ذ	dh
ر	r
ز	Z
س	s
ش	sh
ص	ṣ
ض	ḍ
ط	ṭ
ظ	ẓ
ع	‘
غ	gh
ف	f
ق	q
ل	l
م	m
ن	n
ه	h
و	w
ي	y

Vowels

Short

َ = a | ِ = i | ُ = u

Long

ـا = ā | ـي = ī | ـو = ū

Dipthongs

يْ | *-ay*

وْ | *-aw*

Abbreviation of Companies *and* Financial Institutions

AAOIFI	: Accounting and Auditing Organisation for Islamic Financial Institutions.
DIB	: Dubai Islamic Bank
DJIMI	: Dow Jones Islamic Market Index
HSBC	: Hong Kong Shanghai Banking Corporation
IAIB	: International Association of Islamic Banks
IBB	: Islamic Bank of Britain
ICEIF	: International Centre for Education in Islamic Finance
IDB	: Islamic Development Bank
IFSB	: Islamic Financial Services Board
IIFM	: International Islamic Financial Market
IIFA	: International Islamic Fiqh Academy
IIRA	: The International Islamic Rating Agency
IMF	: International Monetary Fund
OIC	: Organisation of the Islamic Conference
SAC	: Shariah Advisory Council

Abbreviation of Symbols

#	= *ḥadīth* number
v/vv.	= verse/verses
=	= 'equates to'
~	= negation
۞	= end of verse citation
Q.	= al-Qur'ān al-Karīm
s:	Additional comment by author
[...]	Omission of textual segment in a translation
( )	Additional meaning inserted by translator

Table *of* Contents

Transliteration System p.5

Abbreviation of Symbols p.6

Abbreviation of Companies and Financial Systems p.7

Introduction pp.13-14

Chapter 1: The Importance of *Fiqh*: pp.15-22

- The statement if Ibn Ḥajar al-`Asqalānī.
- The statement of Anas b. Mālik.
- The Statement of Imām Mālik.
- The statement of Ibn al-Mubārak.
- The statement of Yaḥyā b. Ma`īn.

Chapter 2: Shariah Advisory Boards (SSB / هيئة الفتاوى و الرقابة الشرعية): pp.23-31

- Role of SSBs.
- Qualifications.
- Prominent International SSB Members.

Chapter 3: Key Notions: ***A Survey*** pp.32-48

- Ribā (الربا).
- Gharar (الغرر).
- Maysir (الميسر).
- Qimār (القمار).
- Dayn (الدين).
- Fraud (الغبن الفاحش).

- Deceit (التدليس).
- Monopoly (الإحتكار).
- Price-fixing (التسعير).
- Selling something one does not have (بيع ما ليس عندك).

Chapter 4: Islamic Contracts: *Outlines* (العقد): pp.49-66

- Outline.
- Definition of the word 'Sale' / البيع.
- Ethics of Sale in Islam.
- Conditions related to the Contracting Parties.
- Conditions related to validity of a Contract.
- Conditions related to the Subject-matter of a Contract.
- Conditions related to the place of the Contract.
- Conditions related to dissolution of a Contract.

Chapter 5: Invalid Contract Types: pp.67-79

- Due to the Contractors.
- Due to the subject of the Sale.
- Due to Ribā.
- Due to Gharar.
- Other invalid contract Types.

Chapter 6: Insurance Contracts (التأمين): pp.80-103

- Conventional Insurance.
- Extended Warranties.

Chapter 7: Forex Trading: (*online*) pp.104-111

- Forex Trading (online/electronic).
- Currency Exchange (الصرف)

Chapter 8: Derivatives Financial Contracts: pp.112-137

- Forward Contracts.
- Futures Contracts.
- Options Trading (الإختيارات).

Chapter 9: Some Financial Schemes: pp.138-176

- Murābaḥa Transactions (Cost-Plus).
- Tawarruq Transactions (reverse Murābaḥa).
- Shariah-Compliant Home Plans:

  1. 'Diminishing *Mushāraka* Scheme' (DMS),
  2. 'Murābaḥa Housing Scheme' (MHS) and
  3. 'Ijāra Muntahiya bi 'l-Tamlīk Programme (IMT)'.

Cost plus housing scheme.

Chapter 10: Islamic Finance: *General Challenges* pp.177-178

Concluding Remarks pp.179-180

Key References p.181

Notes: pp.182-183

Short Glossary pp.183-187

Introducing Islamic Financial Contracts

Introduction

Introduction

This book began originally as a collection of class notes in the form of a booklet for an introduction to newly emerging financial contracts and products. The aim was to present to students a simplified account of key financial transactions in order to assess new financial products or services presented as Shariah-compliant. However, the growth of Shariah finance – beginning in the East and the Middle East and now an attractive part of Western financial institutions[1] – as well as the intricate procedures involved required elaborating integrals of Islamic contract law and transaction law, which thus expanded the booklet beyond a reasonable size. It therefore became necessary to expand on and outline aspects such as what constituted a legally valid contract within Shariah as well as socio-economic aims of contracts in general which is indispensable for evaluating any form of emerging Islamic financial contracts.

There is much that is omitted in this book and it is obvious to the reader that it is neither comprehensive nor is it a detailed work on Islamic finance. It is merely an introduction to key Islamic financial transactions and how some of these contracts are utilised for engineering personal modes of finance and trade-systems for Muslims to engage in. It covers key precepts and elements of Islamic contracts and how they apply to common insurance contracts, derivatives contracts and other financial schemes like home purchasing plans. Each chapter is self-contained and can be read independently of other chapters. Moreover, references

---

[1] See for example David Cameron's recent praise of Islamic finance products announcing his desire to make London the centre for Islamic finance products with an Islamic Index (II) on the London Stock Exchange (LSE); cf. http://www.bbc.co.uk/news/business-24722440. However, one must also be aware of the context in which such unveilings are made, for which see comments at http://www.hizb.org.uk/current-affairs/carrot-and-stick-the-governments-approach-towards-the-muslim-community.

from the original booklet have been considerably updated and more original Arabic material incorporated for familiarity with key source materials as well as for research purposes.

It is hoped therefore that this small contribution is helpful in clarifying existing treatments on Islamic financial contracts as well as an accessible work for non-specialists and general students alike.

s.z.c.

The Importance *of* Learning Fiqh

The Importance of Learning *Fiqh*

1. The Statement of Ibn Ḥajar

2. The Statement of Anas b. Mālik.

3. The Statement of Ibn al-Mubārak.

4. The Statement of Yaḥyā Ibn Ma`īn.

Chapter 1: *The Importance of Learning Fiqh*

———— ♦ ————

***In this Chapter*:**

- Statement of Ibn Ḥajar.
- Statement of Anas Ibn Mālik.
- Statement of Ibn al-Mubārak.
- Statement of Yaḥyā Ibn Ma`īn.

Statement of Ibn Ḥajar:

It is incumbent upon all Muslims to learn the integrals related to their actions in all domains of their life and proceed on this basis. This is the study of 'fiqh' (فقه / 'Islamic positive law' / 'knowledge of Islamic law'). The gálactico of scholars from al-Azhar, the supreme master in ḥadīth scholarship al-Ḥāfiẓ al-Imām Ibn Ḥajar al-`Asqalānī (d.852/1449)[2] comments on the noble *ḥadīth* of the humanity's mercy our blessed Prophet (abundant peace and blessings be upon him): **"Whoever Allah wishes good for, He endows them with knowledge of *fiqh* of the Religion,"** stating:[3]

[...] وفي ذلك بيان ظاهر لفضل العلماء على سائر الناس، ولفضل التفقه في الدين على سائر العلوم...

"...and in this [narration] is a clear exposition of the superiority of the scholars over the rest of the people and the superiority of *fiqh* over all other sciences."[4]

---

[2] For more on him, see A. A. Rahmani, *The Life and Works of Ibn Hajar al-Asqalani*, Islamic Foundation Bangladesh, 2000.

[3] Bukhārī, *Ṣaḥīḥ* (#3116).

[4] Ibn Ḥajar al-`Asqalānī, *Fatḥ al-Bārī*, 1:163-164.

Fiqh[5] ('knowledge of Islamic legal rulings' / 'Islamic positive law') is considered the paramount discipline in Islam, the 'queen of the sciences'. There are many statements of the *Ṣaḥāba* (companions of the Prophet) and early righteous scholars (*al-salaf*) that uphold this for example:

The Statement of Anas b. Mālik:

أنا أبو عبد الله محمد بن عبد الواحد بن أحمد الطرفي المعدل بالكرخ، نا عمر بن إبراهيم بن مردويه الكرخي، نا ابن جعفر النجيرمي، نا أحمد بن سعيد الثقفي، نا أبو روح الهيثم بن برزخ ، نا إبراهيم بن ميسرة عن أنس بن مالك رضي الله عنه، قال : قال رسول الله : إن لكل أمة رهبانية، وإن رهبانية أمتي الجماعات والجمعات وتعليم بعضهم بعضاً شرائع الدين...

"From Anas b. Malik[6] (God be pleased with him) who said: 'every nation has religious leaders and the religious leaders of my community are a group of people who teach each other the obligatory acts (*shara'i`*) of the Religion'."[7]

أنا عبد الغفار بن محمد المؤدب، أنا عمر بن أحمد الواعظ، نا عبد الله بن عمر بن سعيد الطالقاني، نا عمار بن عبد الحميد، نا محمد بن مقاتل الرازي عن أبي العباس جعفر بن هارون عن سمعان بن المهدي عن أنس رضي الله عنه ، قال : قال رسول الله : أفضل العلم الذي يحتاج إليه الناس.

قلت : وأعظم ما بالناس الحاجة إليه من العلوم الفقه فلا علم أفضل منه .

"From Anas b. Mālik (God be pleased with him) who said: The Messenger of God (God bless him and give him peace) said: **'the best knowledge is that which the people need.'**

---

[5] For a discussion of the term 'fiqh', refer to A. Hasan, *The Early Development of Islamic Jurisprudence*, pp.1-11 and I. A. K. Nyazee, *Islamic Jurisprudence*, pp.18-24.

[6] One of the last surviving companions whose life almost bridged the entire seventh century. A profuse transmitter of *ḥadīth* from the Prophet and a highly revered individual. He died in Basra aged over one hundred years. See G. H. A. Juynboll, s.v. *Encyclopaedia of Canonical Ḥadīth*, pp.131-133.

[7] al-Khaṭīb al-Baghdādī, *al-Faqīh wa 'l-Mutafaqqih*, 1:144-145.

I say [s: meaning the author al-Khaṭīb al-Baghdādī]: the greatest science or knowledge the people need is *fiqh* as no science is better or more excellent than it."[8]

فقد روى يحيى بن سليمان عن ابن وهب، قال : سمعت مالكاً يقول : كثير من هذه الأحاديث ضلالة لقد خرجت مني أحاديث لوددت إني ضربت بكل حديث منها سوطين وإني لم أحدث به .

"Yaḥyā b. Sulaymān narrated from Ibn Wahb who said: I heard Mālik [b. Anas][9] say: 'Many of these *ḥadīths* are [a cause for] misguidance;[10] some *hadiths* were narrated by me and I wish that for each of them I had been flogged with a stick twice. I certainly no longer narrate them!'"[11]

حدثنا عبد الرحمن حدثني ابي نا هارون بن سعيد الايلي بمصر قال سمعت ابن وهب – وذكر اختلاف الاحاديث والروايات فقال: لولا اني لقيت مالكا والليث لضللت.

"...Ibn Wahb said regarding the differences over *ḥadīths* and their transmissions that: 'were I not to have met Malik or al-Layth [b. Sa`d], I would surely have been misguided..."[12]

---

[8] al-Khaṭīb al-Baghdādī, *al-Faqīh wa 'l-Mutafaqqih*, 1:145.

[9] One of the early traditionists and jurist of Medina whose compilation entitled *Muwaṭṭa'* is the earliest surviving collection of legal traditions. He developed his own legal methodology comprising one of the four orthodox legal Schools. J. Schacht, "Mālik b. Anas", *EI*[1], 5:205-209.

[10] Meaning they can mislead and cause misunderstanding unless correctly understood.

[11] al-Khaṭīb al-Baghdādī, *al-Faqīh wa 'l-Mutafaqqih*, 2:158.

[12] See Ibn Abī Ḥātim, *al-Jarḥ wa 'l-Ta`dīl*, 1:23; al-Qāḍī `Iyāḍ, *Tartīb al-Madārik*, 2:427; Ibn Ḥibbān, *Kitāb al-Majrūḥīn*, 1:42 (introduction); Ibn Abī Zayd, *al-Jāmi` fī 'l-Sunan*, pp.118-119 and Ibn `Abd al-Barr, *al-Intiqā'*, p.61.

The Statement of Ibn al-Mubārak (d.181/797):

وقال أبو وهب ومحمد بن مزاحم سمعت بن المبارك يقول أفقه الناس أبو حنيفة ما رأيت في الفقه مثله و قال أيضا لولا أن الله تعالى أغاثني بأبي حنيفة وسفيان كنت كسائر الناس...

"Abū Wahb and Muhammad b. Mazāḥim said: I heard Ibn al-Mubārak[13] say: 'The most knowledgeable jurist is Abū Ḥanīfa. I have not seen the likes of him.' [Ibn al-Mubārak] also said: 'If God (Most High) had not rescued me with Abū Ḥanīfa and Sufyān [al-Thawrī][14] I would have been like the rest of the common people'."[15]

The Statement of Yaḥyā Ibn Ma`īn (d.233/847):

وقال أحمد بن علي بن سعيد القاضي سمعت يحيى بن معين يقول سمعت يحيى بن سعيد القطان يقول لا تكذب الله ما سمعنا أحسن من رأى أبي حنيفة وقد أخذنا بأكثر اقواله...

"Aḥmad b. `Alī b. Sa`īd al-Qāḍī said: I heard Yaḥyā b. Ma`īn say: I heard Sa`īd al-Qaṭṭān say: 'We do not belie God. We never heard better than the legal opinions of Abū Ḥanīfa and we followed most of his positions'."[16]

Through *fiqh* therefore, one attains correct knowledge of actions required by the Creator from His servants so that He can correctly worshipped. In Islam, every individual is

[13] A famous ascetic and *mujāhid.* He was also a traditionist of Persian origin as well as a profuse memorizer and collector of *hadith* but saw the pitfalls in attempting to understand them without the requisite legal knowledge. He is said to have compiled approximately 120,000 *ḥadīths.* Cf. al-Subkī's *al-Ṭabaqāt al-Shāfi`iyyat al-Kubrā*, 2:128. See also al-Ṭabarī (trans. E. Landau-Tasseron), *Biographies of the Prophet's Companions and their Successors*, pp.263-264, fn.1170.

[14] Theologian, jurist and famous ascetic of the second century who enjoys immense authority in Islamic pietistic literature as well as traditionist discourse. His reliability is unanimously agreed upon by Muslim scholars as well as his prodigious memory and accuracy. M. Plessner, "Sufyān al-Thawrī", *EI*[1], 7:500-502.

[15] Ibn Ḥajar al- `Asqalānī, *Tahdhīb al-Tahdhīb*, 10:450.

[16] Ibn Ḥajar al- `Asqalānī, *Tahdhīb al-Tahdhīb*, 10:450 and al-Dhahabī, *Tadhkirāt al-Ḥuffāẓ*, 1:307.

duty-bound to learn the integrals related to h/her actions daily and will be in commission of a sin in failing to do so. This includes basic rulings related to buying, selling and general trade, as these are actions people do every day.

`Umar Ibn al-Khaṭṭāb said:

لاَ يَبِعْ فِيْ سُوْقِنَا إِلاَّ مَنْ قَدْ تَفَقَّهَ فِيْ الدِّيْنِ

'No one should sell in our marketplace except those who have attained deep knowledge of the Religion'.[17]

And `Alī Ibn Abī Ṭālib said:

مَنِ اتَّجَرَ قَبْلَ أَنْ يَتَفَقَّهَ ارْتَطَمَ فِيْ الرِّبَا، ثُمَّ ارْتَطَمَ، ثُمَّ ارْتَطَمَ

'Whoever engages in trade before learning will fall further and further into *ribā*...'[18]

Imām al-Ghazālī (d.505/1111)[19] remarked:

كما أنَّه لو كان هذا المسلمُ تاجرًا وقد شاعَ في البلدِ معاملةُ الربا، وجبَ عليهِ تعلُّمُ الحذرِ من الربا، وهذا هو الحقُّ في العلمِ الذي هو فرضُ عينٍ، ومعناه العلمُ بكيفيةِ العملِ الواجبِ

"Likewise, if this Muslim was a merchant and *ribā* was widespread in the land, he must learn about the prohibition on *ribā*. This is knowledge that is an individual obligation, which is knowledge of how to do what is required [...]

---

[17] Tirmidhī, *Sunan* (#487).
[18] As cited in al-Shirbīnī's *al-Mughnī al-Muḥtāj*, 2:22.
[19] Considered one of the greatest thinkers in Islam whose legacy in all aspects of intellectual and spiritual learning influenced the development of Muslim thought as well as its paradigms until the present. His evident contributions include on the one hand a severe critique of Peripatetic philosophy and on the other the complete systematisation of Sufism as an orthodox discipline. See www.ghazali.org for details.

كلُّ عبدٍ هو في مجاري أحوالِه في يومِه وليلتِه لا يخلو من وقائعَ في عبادتِه ومعاملاتِه عن تجددِ لوازمَ عليه، فيلزمُه السؤالُ عن كلِّ ما يقعُ له من النوادرِ، ويلزمُه المبادرةُ إلى تعلُّمِ ما يَتَوَقَّعُ وقوعَه على القربِ غالبًا

Every person in his daily life is bound to face new issues with regard to his worship and dealings with others. So he must ask about everything, whatever new issues he encounters and he must hasten to learn out about what he expects to face before he faces it…"[20]

Therefore, learning the basic rulings related to daily transactions are extremely important in order to avoid falling into usurious dealings or undertaking invalid contracts.

---

[20] al-Ghazālī, *Iḥyā' `Ulūm al-Dīn*, 1:33-34.

Shariah
Supervisory Boards (SSB)

Shariah Supervisory Boards (SSB):

1. Role of SSB Members.

2. Qualifications for SSB Membership.

3. Prominent international SSB Members.

Chapter 2: *Shariah Supervisory Boards* (SSB)

♦

In this chapter

- The role of Shariah boards.
- Qualifications for a SSB scholar.
- Prominent international SSB members.

The Aim and Role of Shariah Boards:

The origin, basis and framework for Islamic banking or financial activities is the Shariah. To ensure that all financial activities conform to Islamic legal injunctions (*aḥkām shar`iyya*), a select panel of specialised Islamic scholars are appointed to supervise or oversee a company's activities. These are known as 'Shariah Supervisory Boards' (SSB) or 'Shariah Supervisory Committees' (SSC) known in Arabic as هيئة الفتاوى و الرقابة الشرعية.[21] The general aims of SSBs include:

---

[21] See for example Y. Abdul-Rahman, *The Art of Islamic Banking and Finance*, pp.61-83; M. T. Skully, "Corporate Governance and Islamic Banks" in *The Foundations of Islamic Banking: Theory, Practice and Education*, ed. M. Ariff et al, pp.105-111; N. Alsayyed, "Shariah Board, The Task of Fatwa and Ijtihad in Islamic Economics and Finance", *MPRA* Paper no.20204, January 2010 available at http://mpra.ub.uni-muenchen.de/20204/1/MPRA_paper_20204.pdf; The Central Bank of Malaysia guidelines for Shariah Committees and financial Institutions, BNM/GPS 1 (2004), "Shariah Boards" available at http://wiki.islamicfinance.de/index.php/Shariah_Board; M. Abdullah, "Analysing the Role of Shariah Advisory Boards in Islamic Financial Institutions", pp.1-14 available at http://papers.ssrn.com and Y. T. DeLorenzo, "Shariah Supervision in Modern Islamic Finance" available at http://www.guidanceresidential.com and idem, "Shariah Supervision of Islamic Mutual Funds", 4th Annual Harvard Forum on Islamic Finance available at http://www.kantakji.com/fiqh/Files/Fatawa/9002.pdf.

1. To maintain transparency in a bank or company's Islamic activity.

2. To 'purify' the transactions, i.e. render them acceptable to Allah.

3. To be part of the financial regulation of Islamic banks or financial institutions.

Below are the key functions and responsibilities of an SSB member:

- To ensure all banking facilities or financial services accord with Islamic values.

- To ensure a bank/company's investment and involvement in projects are operationally Shariah-compliant through for example internal reviews or Shariah audits (cf. fig.1. below).[22]

- To offer practical advice on remedying any non-compliant elements of the company.

- To conduct and guide research into unprecedented financial realities for developing new contracts or financial products and services based on Islamic principles of contract and commercial law.

- To issue or publish legal edicts (*fatāwā*) for review and analyses.

---

[22] For a short reference on Shariah auditing, refer to S. Sultan's *A Mini Guide to Shariah Audit for Islamic Financial Institutions – A Primer*, pp.22-132.

- To publish formal certifications for Shariah-compliant financial products and services.[23]

- The general hierarchy of an SSB is as follows:

A Chairperson of an SSB

↓

A General Secretariat

↓

SSB board member (scholar)	SSB board member (scholar)	SSB board member (scholar)	SSB board member (scholar)

Below is a schema outlining the relationship between an SSB and the entire company:

[23] Based on International Fiqh Academy, Resolution No. 177 (3/19), 2009, pp.6-8. See also Jamaldeen, *Islamic Finance*, pp.261-274 and Kettell, *Islamic Finance*, pp.97-120.

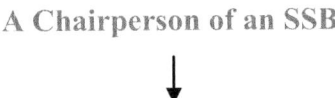

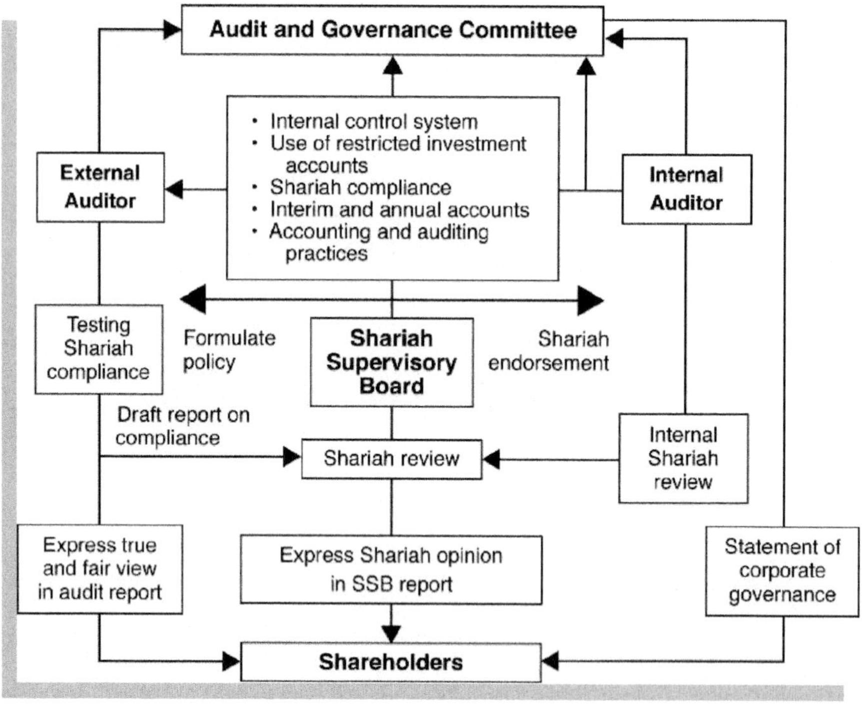

fig.1. a schema of an SSB of a financial institution
(source: *qfinance.com*)

Qualifications:

To become a SSB member, a number of qualifications are stipulated although there are as of yet no formal industry criteria or standards. Some the following include:

1. To be qualified to issue *fatāwā* with legal practice for a number of years.

2. A recognised BA degree and beyond in commercial law or related areas.

3. Knowledge of Arabic (for examination of original legal *fiqh* sources).

4. Academic publications on Islamic Finance or related areas.
5. Authority in the field.
6. Recognition.[24]

Prominent International SSB Members:

Below are snapshot profiles of four SSB members of international repute:

Mufti Taqi Usmani
(1943-)

- Retired judge Appellate Bench, Supreme Court of Pakistan.
- Scholar of the Muslim tradition and chief ideologue of the Deoband Islamic Seminary.
- Deputy Chairman and permanent member of IIFA.
- Member of the SSB for Saudi American Bank, Ahli United Bank (UK), Al-Baraka Group, Jeddah and affiliations to numerous other international Islamic banks.
- Many publications in the field of Islamic finance that are now standard references.

[24] Jamaldeen, *Islamic Finance*, pp.267-270 and Kettel, *Islamic Finance*, pp.107-108.

Dr. Hussain H. Hassan
(1932-)

- A leading specialist in Islamic Law.
- Muslim scholar of the Islamic legal tradition and graduate of the renowned al-Azhar University in Cairo.
- He is instrumental in using Islamic finance as a framework in changing international banks to Islamic ones as well as proposing financial products that are Shariah-compliant.
- He is member and consultant to innumerable SSBs across the Muslim world.
- His publications are numerous and have become standard references in the field.

Dr. Wahba Zuhayli
(1932-)

- A native Syrian scholar and specialist of Islamic law and legal philosophy.
- He is a prodigious author and lecturer and his encyclopaedic works are considered indispensable Muslim legal references for students and specialists.
- He is advisor to many international SSBs.

Dr. Yusuf T. DeLorenzo
(1948-)

- A renowned scholar, translator and speaker on Islamic transactional law and general Muslim issues.
- He studied in the USA, Pakistan and elsewhere with affiliations to traditional Islamic learning circles.
- He has advised banks and organisations like the ADB and IFSB on asset management, financial operations and was instrumental in the subsequent development of international *sukuk* bonds.
- He has been a member of ISRA, ICEIF and AAOIFI and has numerous other affiliations with financial institutions.
- His many publications are important references in the field of Islamic finance and commercial law.

There are many other Islamic finance specialists of equal repute including but not restricted to:

1. Dr. Yūsuf al-Qaraḍāwī.
2. Dr. Muḥammad al-Qārī b. `Īd.
3. Dr. Daud Bakar.
4. Dr. `Abd Allāh b. `Abd al-`Azīz al-Muṣliḥ.
5. Sh. `Abd Allāh b. Sulaymān al-Manīya.
6. Sh. Niẓām M. S. Ya`qūbī.[25]

---

[25] List from Kettell, *Islamic Finance*, pp.108-114.

Key Notions: *A Survey*

Key Notions: *A Survey*

1. Ribā (الربا).
2. Gharar (الغرر).
3. Maysir (الميسر).
4. Qimār (القمار).
5. Dayn (الدين).
6. Fraud (الغبن الفاحش).
7. Deceit (التدليس).
8. Monopoly (الإحتكار).
9. Price-fixing (التسعير).
10. Selling something one does not have (بيع ما ليس عندك).

Chapter 3: Key Notions: *A Survey*

In this Chapter:

- Ribā (الربا).
- Gharar (الغرر).
- Maysir (الميسر).
- Qimār (القمار).
- Dayn (الدين).
- Criminal Fraud (الغبن الفاحش).
- Deceit (التدليس).
- Monopoly (الإحتكار).
- Price-fixing (التسعير).
- Selling something one does not have (بيع ما ليس عندك).

Below are a number of key concepts within Islamic Law – developed in detail by Muslim scholars – that underpin financial Islamic contracts and restrict the modes of finance and instruments available to traders, investors and financial companies. They are impermissible ways to acquire ownership of something and thus unlawful. Any contract that contains one of these precepts as an essential element will not be Shariah-compliant and will render that contract either void or invalid pending elimination of the respective element. Each of these precepts or notions is amplified with examples in successive chapters and so below is just a short survey for providing a framework.

Ribā (الربا): Usually translated as 'interest' or 'usury'. In Arabic, it means 'surplus', 'increase' and 'gain'.[26] In Islamic

[26] al-Zuḥaylī, *al-Fiqh al-Islāmī*, 5:351:

Law, it refers to an unwarranted gain, i.e. an increase without a share in risk or liability which thus renders it unjustified.[27] This is categorically prohibited in Shariah. Foundational texts of Islam are explicit on this. Allah states: {*And Allah has permitted trade but prohibited ribā…*}.[28]

وأحل الله البيع وحرم الربا...۝

The Prophet declared *ribā* prohibited as reported from `Alī who heard him say: "**…cursed is the one who consumes interest, deals in interest, records interest, abstains from paying Zakat and he used to prohibit excessive mourning**."[29]

و عن علي انه سمع رسول الله صلي الله عليه و سلم لعن اكل الربوا و موكله و كاتبه و مانع الصدقة و كان ينهي عن النوح

A person cannot benefit from *ribā* nor be involved in it in any way whether through transaction or employment[30]

الربا في اللغة: الزيادة، قال الله تعالى: {فإذا أنزلنا عليها الماء اهتزت وربت} [الحج:22/5] أي زادت ونمت، وقال سبحانه: {أن تكون أمة هي أربى من أمة} [النحل:16/92] أي أكثر عدداً، يقال: (أربى فلان على فلان) أي زاد عليه .

[27] Ibid., 5:351:

وهو في الشرع: الزيادة في أشياء مخصوصة، وهذا تعريف الحنابلة. وعرفه في الكنز عند الحنفية بأنه: فضل مال بلا عوض في معاوضة مال بمال. ويقصد به فضل مال ولو حكماً، فيشمل التعريف حينئذ ربا النسيئة والبيوع الفاسدة، باعتبار أن الأجل في أحد العوضين فضل حكمي بلا عوض مادي محسوس، والأجل يبذل بسببه عادة عوض زائد

[28] Q. 2:275 and 278-279 as well as 3:130.

[29] al-Ṭabrīzī, *Mishkāt al-Maṣābīḥ* (#2829).

[30] See my *Introducing the Fiqh of Employment* for details on this as well as employment scenarios. It is reported as being Imām Abū Ḥanīfa's position that he and Imām Ḥasan al-Shaybānī permitted receiving interest from non-Muslims only in *dār al-ḥarb* (non-Islamic territories = a land primarily described as the political authority belonging to non-Muslims):

Ibn `Ābidīn, *Radd al-Muḥtār*, 5:186:

(قوله ولا بين حربي ومسلم مستأمن) احترز بالحربي عن المسلم الأصلي والذمي، وكذا عن المسلم الحربي إذا هاجر إلينا ثم عاد إليهم، فإنه ليس للمسلم أن يرابي معه اتفاقا كما يذكره الشارح، ووقع في البحر هنا غلط حيث قال: وفي المجتبى مستأمن منا باشر مع رجل مسلما كان أو ذميا في دراهم أو من أسلم هناك شيئا من العقود التي لا تجوز فيما بيننا كالربويات وبيع الميتة جاز عندهما خلافا لأبي يوسف اه

al-Sarakhsī, *al-Mabsūṭ*, 14:98:

قال رحمه الله: ذكر عن مكحول عن رسول الله صلى الله عليه وسلم قال: "لا ربا بين المسلمين وبين أهل دار الحرب في دار الحرب" وهذا الحديث وإن كان مرسلا فمكحول فقيه ثقة والمرسل من مثله مقبول وهو دليل لأبي حنيفة ومحمد رحمهما الله في جواز بيع المسلم الدرهم بالدرهمين من الحربي في دار الحرب وعند أبي يوسف والشافعي رحمهما الله لا يجوز

al-Bukhārī, *al-Muḥīt al-Burhānī*, 10:489:

إذا دخل المسلم دار الحرب بأمان أو بغير أمان وعقد مع حربي عقد الربا بأن اشترى درهما بدرهمين أو اشترى درهما بدينار إلى أجل أو باع منهم خمرا أو خنزيرا أو ميتة أو دما بمال قال أبو حنيفة ومحمد ذلك كله جائز وقال أبو يوسف لا يجوز من المسلم وأهل الحرب في دار الحرب إلا ما يجوز من المسلمين

Ibn Nujaym, *al-Baḥr al-Rā'iq*, 6:147:

قوله (ولا بين الحربي والمسلم ثمة) أي لا ربا بينهما في دار الحرب عندهما خلافا لأبي يوسف

al-Zayla`ī, *Tabyīn al-Ḥaqā'iq*, 4:97:

قال رحمه الله (وبين الحربي والمسلم ثمة) أي لا ربا بينهما في دار الحرب وكذلك إذا تبايعا بيعا فاسدا في دار الحرب فهو جائز وهذا عند أبي حنيفة ومحمد وقال أبو يوسف والشافعي لا يجوز

al-Kasānī, *al-Badā'i` al-Ṣanā'i`*, 4:16:

وعلى هذا الأصل يخرج ما إذا دخل مسلم دار الحرب تاجرا فباع حربيا درهما بدرهمين أو غير ذلك من سائر البيوع الفاسدة في حكم الإسلام أنه يجوز عند أبي حنيفة ومحمد وعند أبي يوسف لا يجوز (بدائع الصنائع

al-Fatāwā al-Hindiyya, 3:248:

because it is not permissible to benefit from something prohibited.

***ribā al-faḍl/ribā 'l-buyū`*** (ربا الفضل / ربا البيوع): In all types of trade as well as the *Salam* contract, only six items are usurious (*al-amwāl al-ribawiyya*) and whatever falls under their ruling (i.e. in description and genus). These items are mentioned in the *ḥadīth* from `Ubāda b. al-Ṣāmit:[31]

لا تبيعوا الذَّهبَ بالذَّهبِ ولا الورِقَ بالورِقِ ولا البُرَّ بالبُرِّ ولا الشَّعيرَ بالشَّعيرِ ولا التَّمرَ بالتَّمرِ ولا الملحَ بالملحِ إلَّا سواءً بسواءٍ عينًا بعينٍ يدًا بيدٍ ولكن بيعوا الذَّهبَ بالورِقِ والورِقَ بالذَّهبِ والبرَّ بالشَّعيرِ والشَّعيرَ بالبرِّ والتَّمرَ بالملحِ والملحَ بالتَّمرِ يدًا بيدٍ كيفَ شئتُمْ ...

"Do not sell gold for gold, silver for silver, wheat for wheat, barley for barley, date for date and salt for salt, except like for like and hand to hand..."[32]

Dates	**Wheat**	**Barley**
Gold	**Silver**	**Salt**

If each of these items are exchanged, they must only be of the same quantity (weight and volume) and on the spot (immediate exchange) without deferring to a later date, e.g. 1 kg of silver must be exchanged with 1kg of silver, hand in hand in the same place of exchange. However, if any one of these items are exchanged with each other, then equivalence is not necessary, e.g. if 1kg of wheat is exchanged for 2kg of barley is permitted as long as they are hand to hand, i.e.

دخل مسلم أو ذمي دار الحرب بأمان أو بغيره وعقد مع الحربي عقد الربا بأن اشترى درهما بدرهمين أو درهما بدينار إلى أجل معلوم أو باع منهم خمرا أو خنزيرا أو ميتة أو دما بمال فذلك كله جائز عند الطرفين وقال القاضي لا يجوز بين المسلم والحربي ثمة إلا ما يجوز بين المسلمين

[31] See al-Nabhānī, *The Economic System in Islam*, pp.245-248.
[32] See *Mishkāt al-Maṣābīḥ* of al-Ṭabrīzī (= the *takhrīj* of Ibn Ḥajar's *Hidāyat al-Ruwāt*), 3:151.

immediate and on the spot. Moreover, trading foodstuffs for a deferred monetary price does not fall under the purview of *ribā*.

ribā al-nasī'a (ربا النسيئة): On any loan or borrowings (*qaraḍ*), *ribā* applies when a higher or lower return is stipulated, *ex ante*, from the principle whether for the 6 items mentioned above or anything else the ownership of which is lawfully transferable.[33]

There are a number of reasons for Islam eliminating *ribā* from transactions and they include:

1. To avoid injustice (*ẓulm*) against one of the contracting parties, whether borrower or lender, e.g. financier will receive surplus or gain without any risk or loss on his part.

2. To avoid adverse impacts on society in terms of bad lending practice, creation of anxiety due to insurmountable debt levels, exploitation of the weak and financially vulnerable (cf. loan sharks and exorbitant interest rates in 'predatory lending'). In this way, *ribā* is demeaning to the human personality.

---

[33] Ibn `Ābidīn, *Radd al-Muḥtār*, 5:169:

لان الربا هو الفضل الخالي عن العوض

"…because *ribā* is a surplus gained without any form of compensation." There are a number of dangerous consequences of *ribā* discussed by Muslim scholars for which see Kettell, *Islamic Finance*, pp.16-21; Jamaldeen, *Islamic Finance*, pp.16-17; M. El-Gamal, "An Economic Explication of the Prohibition of *Ribā* in Classical Islamic Jurisprudence", pp.1-20; Daud Bakar, "Riba and Islamic Banking and Finance", pp.1-23; N. Schoon, *Islamic Banking and Finance*, pp.19-21; M. Abdul Aziz, "The Negative Impact of Riba Banking on the Performance of Islamic Banking in Dual Banking System" (MSc thesis submitted to the IIUM, 2012), pp.31-36; A. Khorshid, *Islamic Insurance: A Modern Approach to Islamic Banking*, pp.31-43; M. S. Netzer, "Riba in Islamic Jurisprudence: The Role of 'Interest' in Discourse on Law and State" (MA thesis submitted to The Fletcher School, 2004), pp.7-12 and al-Zuḥaylī, *Financial Transactions*, 1:337-352.

3. To avoid ruin (*mahq*) because *ribā* is a means to destruction and destabilisation of society and the economy (cf. the various economic crises in the world due to not only fractional reserve banking [making money out of nothing] but the net interest income).[34]

Gharar (الغرر): The Prophet explicitly forbade *gharar*. Abū Hurayra relates that '…the Prophet forbade *gharar*…'[35]

عن أبي هريرة قال نهي رسول الله عن بيع الحصاة وعن بيع الغرر

The word is often translated into English from the Arabic as 'uncertainty', 'risk', 'hazard' and 'ambiguity'. Linguistically, it means 'danger' or 'risk' (*khaṭar*) – particularly one that is unknown or intolerable (meaning avoidable or excessive).[36] In the terminology of the jurists, it refers to:

---

[34] See for example "Australia: Financial Stability Assessment", IMF Country Report No.12/308 (Nov. 2012), pp.10-11 that alludes to net interest margins as a cause of the financial problem. See http://www.apra.gov.au/AboutAPRA/Publications/Documents/cr12308%5B1%5D.pdf. Cf. also Z. Abd al-Rahman, "Riba (Usury): Today's Practical Form and the Reasons Behind its Prohibition" available at http://www.kantakji.com/fiqh/Files/Riba/gabungan.htm

[35] Muslim, *Ṣaḥīḥ* (#3170).

[36] al-Azharī defines it as:

قال الأزهري: ويدخل في بيع الغرر البيوع المجهولة

"…what is included in *gharar* is transaction of things that are unknown…" See Ibn Fāris *Mu`jam Maqāyīs al-Lugha*, 4:380-381; Ibn Manẓūr, *Lisān al-`Arab*, 6:317 and E. W. Lane, *Arabic-English Lexicon*, Bk. II, p.2239. al-Nawawī said in *Sharḥ Ṣaḥīḥ Muslim*:

وَأَمَّا النَّهْي عَنْ بَيْع الْغَرَر فَهُوَ أَصْل عَظِيم مِنْ أُصُول كِتَاب الْبُيُوع. وَيَدْخُل فِيهِ مَسَائِل كَثِيرَة غَيْر مُنْحَصِرَة، كَبَيْعِ الْمَعْدُوم وَالْمَجْهُول وَبَيْع الْحَمْل فِي الْبَطْن. وَكُلّ هَذَا بَيْعه بَاطِل لأَنَّهُ غَرَر مِنْ غَيْر حَاجَة

As for the prohibition on *gharar* transactions, this is one of the important principles in the section on financial transactions and includes

[1] A transaction whose consequences or outcome is not known.[37]

[2] Something not known in the future.[38]

[3] Something that has two outcomes with the more severe or worse outcome being more likely.[39]

---

innumerable legal issues such as selling non-existent items or unknown ones, or selling an animal that is still in the womb. All such transactions are invalid because it is *gharar* that could be avoided…"

In *al-Mawsū`at al-Fiqhiyya*, 31:151 it states:

يشترط في الغرر حتى يكون مؤثراً أن يكون كثيرا أما إذا كان الغرر يسيرا فإنه لا تأثير له على العقد، قال القرافي: الغرر والجهالة – أي في البيع – ثلاثة أقسام: كثير ممتنع إجماعا كالطير في الهواء وقليل جائز إجماعا كأساس الدار وقطن الجبة، ومتوسط اختلف فيه هل يلحق بالأول أم بالثاني؟ وقال ابن رشد الحفيد: الفقهاء متفقون على أن الغرر الكثير في المبيعات لا يجوز، وأن القليل يجوز

"One of the conditions of *gharar* is that the unknown element must be considerable or great. However, if the unknown element is slight, then it does not affect the transaction. And al-Qarāfī said: *gharar* and *jahāla* – i.e., in buying and selling – are of three types: [2] a considerable degree which is forbidden according to consensus, such as selling birds in the air; [2] a small amount which is permissible according to consensus such as the foundations of a house or cotton filling of a quilted garment. However, there is a difference of opinion concerning [the third type] which is the moderate amount and whether it is regarded as the former or the latter? Ibn Rushd said: the jurists are agreed that a large degree of *gharar* in transactions is not allowed and that a little is permissible…"

[37] See al-Sarakhsī, *al-Mabsūṭ*, 12:194:

الغرر: ما يكون مستور العاقبة

[38] See *al-Furūq*, 3:265 of al-Qarāfī:

هو الذي لا يدرى هل يحصل أم لا كالطير في الهواء والسمك في الماء

[39] See al-Isnawī, *Nihayāt al-Sūl*, 2:89:

الغرر: هو ما تردد بين شيئين أغلبهما أخوفهما

[4] Trading in unknown counter-values (e.g. seller does not know what he is selling and the buyer does not know what he is buying).[40]

Thus, *gharar* transactions have no known or defined elements within the contract that therefore hinders the following from taking place:

1. An informed decision about what to trade, buy/sell on the part of both contractual parties.
2. Correct disclosure of important information.
3. Knowledge of the outcomes of a transaction.
4. Control over the contract or transaction.
5. Justice between parties (as one party may have an advantage over another due to this ambiguity).
6. Amicable trading and exchanges (free from animosity).

The remedy for *gharar* is simply to define the essential terms of a contract without vagueness or ambiguity, e.g. the object of sale, the description of the sale items, time of delivery, wage, quantity, price, etc.[41]

Maysir (الميسر): 'Games of chance', 'gambling'. A generic mode of gain that does not involve earning or legitimate effort.[42] It is seen by some as synonymous with *qimār*[43] and

---

[40] See Ibn Ḥazm, *al-Muḥallā*, 8:396:

ما لا يدري المشتري ما اشترى، أو البائع ما باع

[41] al-Zuḥaylī, *Financial Transactions*, 1:80-87; Schoon, *Islamic Banking and Finance*, pp.22-23 and Kamali, *Islamic Commercial Law*, pp.84-98.
[42] Kamali, *Islamic Commercial Law*, p.151.
[43] Ibid., p.152.

is categorically prohibited in the Qur'an: {*Indeed, intoxicants, gambling, idols and divination by arrows are filthy and handiwork of Satan so keep well clear of it if you want to be successful...*}.

يَا أَيُّهَا الَّذِينَ آمَنُواْ إِنَّمَا الْخَمْرُ وَالْمَيْسِرُ وَالأَنصَابُ وَالأَزْلاَمُ رِجْسٌ مِّنْ عَمَلِ الشَّيْطَانِ فَاجْتَنِبُوهُ لَعَلَّكُمْ تُفْلِحُونَ ۝

Qimār (القمار): Often translated as 'gambling' or 'speculation' and overlaps with the word *maysir*. This is categorically forbidden in Shariah as it involves possession of something dependent on the occurrence of some uncertain event, i.e. based on luck or mere chance as opposed to investment and entrepreneurial considerations.[44] By implication, it extends to any agreement or deal where there is definite loss for one party and definite gain for another party without specifying which party will gain and which will lose.[45]

Dayn: Sale of debts (بيع الدين بالدين): The consensus recorded in *fiqh* books is that the Prophet prohibited the sale of a debt with a debt (postponed credit) as reported by Ibn `Umar: **"The Prophet forbade *al-kāli' bi 'l-kāli'*..."**[46]

نهى عن بيع الكالئ بالكالئ

---

[44] Ibid., pp.151-157. Abū Bakr al-Jaṣṣāṣ states in *al-Aḥkām al-Qur'ān*, 2:465:

ولا خلاف بين أهل العلم في تحريم القمار

"And there is no disagreement among the people of knowledge regarding the prohibition of *qimār*..." cf. also F. Rosenthal, *Gambling in Islam*, pp.67-112 for an account from early sources.

[45] Kettell, *Islamic Finance*, p.223 and A. Ahmed, *Theory and Practice of Modern Islamic Finance*, pp.99-100.

[46] Narrated by al-Daraquṭnī in his *Sunan* although see al-Shawkanī's discussion on the reliability of the narration in *Nayl al-Awṭār*, 5:156. Cf. Kamali, *Islamic Commercial Law*, pp.125-130 and al-Zuḥaylī, *Financial Transactions*, 1:78-79.

The sale of one debt for another debt is when both counter-values (price and item) in a contract are deferred to a later delivery date. Thus, the seller is not made the owner of the price and the buyer owner of the item of sale at the time the sale is being conducted which is the requirement in Islamic contracts.

Fraud (الغبن الفاحش): Fraud (*ghubn*) is strictly prohibited in Islam and the many statements from the Prophet are clear regarding it:

من بايعتَ فقل: لا خِلابة

"Whoever trades with you, say: 'there is no deceit'..."[47]

Linguistically, it is synonymous with deceiving and involves lying or false representation, e.g. in the price of something.[48] It is wrongful or criminal deception intended to result in financial gain where the scale of deception is evident or large.[49] Thus, *ghubn* is not the same as bargaining or negotiating a price, which is permissible as it is a form of skill in negotiation and excludes as well a genuine ignorance whether of prices or commodities.[50] What is considered to be 'criminal' or 'serious' fraud (*fāḥish*) is what the traders (*tujjār*) in that locality consider to be so. So price misrepresentation would be ascertained or judged by local traders in local markets and not necessarily by some fraction (¼, ⅓, ½, etc.) or some determined % of the commodity value (e.g. 10%, 15%, 20%, etc.).[51]

---

[47] Muslim, *Ṣaḥīḥ* (#1533).
[48] al-Nabhānī, *The Economic System in Islam*, p.176.
[49] Ibid., p.177.
[50] Ibid., p.177.
[51] Ibid., pp.177-178.

Deceit (التدليس): Islam forbids, deception, cheating and lying. Scholars have given some definitions of cheating (*al-ghish*) and deceit as follows:

[1] al-Munāwī:

الغش ما يخلط الرديء بالجيد.

"...cheating is mixing bad with good."

[2] al-Haythamī:

الغش المحرم أن يعلم ذو السلعة من نحو بائع أو مشتر فيها شيئاً لو اطلع مريد أخذها ما أخذ بذلك المقابل

"...and the forbidden type of cheating is when the owner of the goods knows something which, if the would-be purchaser (*al-murīd*) knew about it, he would not pay that amount of money for it..."[52]

Deceit is the deliberate practice of concealing the truth about some aspect of the contract (e.g. the product, price, delivery, etc.) or misrepresentation of facts regarding it.[53] It also removes blessings from a contract and is a means for heavy legal sanction if conviction is proven.[54]

Both fraud and deceit hinder the following from taking place in transactions:

---

[52] al-Haythamī, *al-Zawājir*, 1:239.
[53] al-Nabhānī, *The Economic System in Islam*, p.178.
[54] Ibid., p.179. Interestingly, some scholars have attributed one cause for subjugation of the Muslim *ummah* to non-Muslim authority being illicit modes of transaction as well as cheating and deception in trade. See al-Haythamī, *al-Zawājir*, 1:239:

ولهذه القبائح – أي الغش – التي ارتكبها التجار والمتسببون وأرباب الحرف والبضائع سلط الله عليهم الظلمة فأخذوا أموالهم، وهتكوا حريمهم، وبل وسلط عليهم الكفار فأسروهم واستعبدوهم، وأذاقوهم العذاب والهوان ألواناً

1. Honest trade and dealings, which is required by Islamic ethics of trade.
2. Amicable and smooth trading free from animosity, which is what the Shariah seeks to instil.
3. Accuracy and symmetry in transactions.
4. Ethical trading.

Monopoly (الإحتكار): this is categorically prohibited in Islam based on the Prophet's statement: **"no-one monopolises except the wrongdoer..."**[55]

لا يَحْتَكِرُ إِلَّا خاطِئٌ

Linguistically, it refers to hoarding something to sell it for a higher price.[56] Controlling the possession and supply of or trade of commodities is strictly forbidden and the Shariah seeks to eliminate this as part of commerce.[57] Monopoly also involves blocking the means of accessing specific commodities in order to exploit the rise in price due to its demand or need in the people.[58]

Price-fixing (التسعير): the Shariah does not specify that commodities of trade have to have a specific price but only that the contractual parties consent to a price.[59] In the Khilāfah, the Khalīfah or his official deputy cannot force a certain price for traders to adopt.[60] If prices fluctuate due to lack of goods or their unavailability, it is the duty of the Khalīfah to ensure they are available in order to stabilise prices. This is what `Umar Ibn al-Khaṭṭāb did in the year of famine in Ḥijāz; he imported required commodities from

---

[55] Muslim, *Ṣaḥīḥ* (#1605).
[56] al-Nabhānī, *The Economic System in Islam*, p.181.
[57] Ibid., pp.180-181.
[58] Ibid., p.181.
[59] Ibid., pp.182-183.
[60] Ibid., p.183.

Egypt and al-Shām that eventually stabilised the price without the need to fix them.[61]

Monopolies are dangerous because:

1. Sole control of the supply and production of commodities (to decrease its availability and thus inflate demand for it) by a single Company means one can fix prices and control it (cf. gas and electricity prices by energy companies). Islam seeks to avoid both control of commodities and price-fixing as this leads to injustice and one of the aims in Shariah is to remove injustice and unjust practices.[62]

Selling something one does not have (بيع ما ليس عندك): This is based on the following statement of the Prophet:

لا يحلُّ سلفٌ وبيعٌ، ولاَ شرطانِ في بيعٍ، ولاَ بيعُ ما لم يَضمَنْ، ولاَ بيعُ ما ليسَ عندَكَ

---

[61] Ibid., p.184 as well as Ahmad, *Theory and Practice*, pp.100-101. There is some juristic disagreement over fixing prices within the traditional *fiqh* literature. Some contemporary scholars have argued for the need to have a price benchmark that adjusts/fixes prices of commodities in the markets in order to circumvent injustice, manipulation and exploitation using as evidence juristic precedence, public utility (*maṣlaḥa*) as well as *maqāṣid al-sharīʿa* reasoning. For details, refer to the discussion in "Islamic Pricing Benchmark", *International Shariah Research Academy*, Research Paper, no. 16 (2010), pp.4-23.

[62] See M. A. al-Zarqa, "Monopoly and Monopolistic Markets" in *Encyclopaedia of Islamic Economics,* vol.2, ed. by M. Kahf, pp.97-105 and "Prophetic Prohibition against Economic Monopolies" available at http://www.islamweb.net. It is for this reason that there are a cluster of sales that are prohibited in Islam, in order to protect the traders' rights such as intercepting caravan *en route* to markets in order to exploit the seller's ignorance of the local prices or to sell to a Bedouin who has no knowledge of town or city trading prices and thus also exploited by local buyers. See A. Hassan, *Early Islamic Commercial Law*, pp.32-34.

"It is not permissible to combine *salaf* with a sale, nor two transactions in the same sale, nor to gain something without liability nor a sale of what you do not have…"[63]

Thus, a condition in Islamic contracts is that a seller is not permitted to sell what he does not own.[64] If a seller has no legal entitlement or established ownership of something, he may not sell it. Related to this condition is that of possession (*qabḍ*). In other words, the seller must have either *actual* possession (*qabḍ ḥaqīqī*) or *constructive* possession (*qabḍ ḥukmī*) of what he is selling in order to legally transfer the ownership of the item in a sale. It also implies that in order to further sell an item that was already purchased, possession is required to make a subsequent sale of that item.[65]

Thus, in conclusion, Shariah seeks to enable the following when it comes to transactions:

1. Elimination of animosity and acrimony between contractual parties.

---

[63] Abū Dāwud, *Sunan* (#3504) and Tirmidhī, *Sunan* (#1234). Imām Badr a-Dīn al-`Aynī comments on this type of transaction and explains the reasoning behind the prohibition:

مَعْنَاهُ: أَن يَشْتَرِي من إِنْسَان طَعَاما بدرهم إِلى أجل ثمَّ يَبِيعهُ مِنْهُ أَو من غَيره قبل أَن يقبضهُ بِدِرْهَمَيْنِ مثلا، فَلَا يجوز لِأَنَّهُ فِي التَّقْدِير: بيع دِرْهَم بدرهم، وَالطَّعَام غَائِب، فَكَأَنَّهُ قد بَاعه درهمه الَّذِي اشْتَرِي بِهِ الطَّعَام بِدِرْهَمَيْنِ، فَهُوَ ربا، لِأَنَّهُ بيع غَائِب بناجز فَلَا يَصح

"What this means is: If he buys some foodstuffs from a person for one dirham to be delivered later, then he sells it back to him or to someone else before taking possession of it for two dirhams, for example, that is not permissible because it is in effect selling cash for cash, when the food is not there. So, it is as if he sold his dirham with which he brought the food for two dirhams, which is *ribā*, because it is selling something that is not there for cash. Hence, to do this is not valid…" `*Umdat al-Qārī*, 11:250:

[64] Kamali, *Islamic Commercial Law*, pp.110-116.

[65] Ibid., pp.117-124.

2. Elimination of ambiguity and vagueness in contract details.

3. Elimination of speculation in trading.

4. Elimination of any usurious elements.

5. Elimination of monopoly and barriers to trade.

6. Establish honesty and correct representation in trading practice.

7. Establish knowledge symmetry.

8. Establish real ownership.

9. Establish correct transfer of assets.

The Islamic Contract: *Outlines*

The Islamic Contract: *Outlines*

1. Outlines.
2. Definition of the word 'Sale' / البيع.
3. Ethics of Sale in Islam.
4. Conditions related to the Contracting Parties.
5. Conditions related to validity of a Contract.
6. Conditions related to the Subject-matter of a Contract.
7. Conditions related to the place of the Contract.
8. Conditions related to Contractual Options (الخيار).
9. Conditions related to dissolution of a Contract.

Chapter 4: *The Islamic Contract* (العقد)

In this Chapter:

- Outline.
- Definition of the word البيع.
- Ethics of Sale in Islam.
- Conditions related to the Contracting Parties.
- Conditions related to validity of a Contract.
- Conditions related to the Subject-matter of a Contract.
- Conditions related to the place of the Contract.
- Conditions related to Contractual Options (الخيار).
- Conditions related to dissolution of a Contract.

Outline:

Allah permitted trade, which is a system that enables human beings to gain their worldly interests (*maṣāliḥ*) and needs.[66] It is also a means of increasing ownership of things.[67] Islamic contract law is a rich but complex area of study.[68] It is imperative to understand the basic components of contracts according to the Shariah so that contemporary contracts – whether sale contracts or financial contracts – can be measured according to Shariah legal rubrics.

---

[66] al-Nabhānī, *The Economic System in Islam*, p.132.

[67] Ibid., pp.132-133.

[68] See F. E. Vogel and S. L. Hayes, *Islamic Law and Finance: Religion, Risk and Return*, pp.97-128; H. Visser, *Islamic Finance: Principles and Practice*, pp.75-80; A. Hassan, *Sales and Contracts in Early Islamic Commercial Law*, ch.5-7, pp.36-85; A. Kharofa, *Transactions in Islamic Law*, pp.1-22 and O. Arabi, *Studies in Modern Islamic Law and Jurisprudence*, pp.39-63.

Below are general conditions pertaining to contracts particularly those of buying and selling (*buyū`*).

The key areas discussed by the jurists (*fuqahā'*) that relate to contracts include:

The Pillar of the Contract (*al-rukn*):

1. The Offer and Acceptance (*ījāb wa qabūl*).

The Conditions of the Contract (*sharā'it*):

2. The contractors (*al-`āqid*).
3. The conditions of validity (*ṣiḥḥa*).
4. The conditions of the subject matter/object of the contract (*ma`qūd `alayh*).
5. The conditions of the place of the contract (*al-majlis*).

The Definition of the word "*bay`*" (البيع):

- Imām al-Mawṣilī explains the meaning of 'sale' as follows:

البيع في اللغة : مطلق المبادلة، وكذلك الشراء، سواء كانت في مال أو غيره . قال الله تبارك وتعالى : إن الله اشترى من المؤمنين أنفسهم وأموالهم وقال تعالى : أولئك الذين اشتروا الضلالة بالهدى فما ربحت تجارتهم وما كانوا مهتدين وفي الشرع : مبادلة المال المتقوم بالمال المتقوم تمليكا وتملكا، فإن وجد تمليك المال بالمنافع فهو إجارة أو نكاح، وإن وجد مجانا فهو هبة، وهو عقد مشروع

"The word *bay`* linguistically means 'a general exchange of some commodity or other'. This is also the linguistic meaning of *al-shirā'* [...] According to the legal definition, it is: 'an exchange of two commodities that involves transfer of ownership.' If the usufruct of the commodity is owned, it would be an *ijāra* contract or a marriage contract whereas if it is free it would be a gift contract which is permitted..."[69]

From this, the following is inferred:

- A contract (*`aqd*) is an exchange (*mubādala*) of one commodity with another (i.e. price with an item).
- The commodity (*māl*) has to be something desirable (*marghūb*).
- The commodity has to be something beneficial that satisfies a need and requirement of people.
- The commodity cannot be something unbeneficial (e.g. dust, faeces, etc.).

The *ḥukm*, Price and Object of contracts:

- Contracts have a *purpose* or *aim* which is known as the *ḥukm* (الحكم).[70] This refers to what is sought in the contract, which is the buyer's ownership of the object and the seller's ownership of the price.

Ethics of sale in Islamic Law:[71]

1. **Avoiding excessive profits**: Islam is not against generation of profit but excessive profit at the expense and disadvantage of buyers is undesirable.

2. **Complete disclosure**: there must be full disclosure of all relevant information pertaining to the contract in order to avoid a form of misrepresentation informational asymmetry.

---

[69] al-Mawṣilī, *al-Ikhtiyār li-Ta`līl al-Mukhtār*, 2:243 and al-Nabhānī, *al-Shakhṣiyya al-Islāmiyya*, 2:284.
[70] al-Taftazānī, *al-Talwīḥ Sharḥ al-Tawḍīḥ*, 2:122.
[71] See al-Zuḥaylī, *Islamic Financial Transactions*, 1:7-8.

3. **Ease of conduct**: the negotiations of a contract must not be too hard, excessive or demanding. It must not be aggressive and with ill feeling or rancour. This is undesirable.

4. **Oaths**: There should be an avoidance of making oaths in the name of Allah when conducting and concluding contracts.[72]

5. **Paying charity**: traders and merchants ought to offer regular charity (*ṣadaqa*) in order to purify the money from any shortcoming, failings and bad practice.

6. **Documentation of debts/sales**: It is desirable that all contracts and loans be written down and documented – especially loans and debts.[73]

The Pillar of a Contract:

- Imām al-Kasānī explains:

وأما ركن البيع : فهو مبادلة شيء مرغوب بشيء مرغوب وذلك قد يكون بالقول وقد يكون بالفعل (أما) القول فهو المسمى بالإيجاب والقبول في عرف الفقهاء ... وأما المبادلة بالفعل فهي التعاطي ويسمى هذا البيع بيع المراوضة

"The pillar (*rukn*) of the sales contract is exchanging two desired things which can either be through verbal exchange or physical exchange. If it is a verbal exchange, then in the common terminology of the jurists it is called 'offer and acceptance' […] and if it is a physical exchange, it is called a 'give and take sale' and is also known as the *murāwaḍa* sale…"[74]

---

[72] Based on Q. 2:224.
[73] Based on Q. 2:282.
[74] al-Kasānī, *al-Badā'i` al-Ṣanā'i`*, 5:134-136.

The Pillar of the Contract:

[1] **Offer and acceptance (*al-ījāb wa 'l-qabūl*)**: this is the 'pillar' (*rukn*) of the contract where a mutual exchange occurs between two parties (= *reciprocity*) free from coercion, fraud or misrepresentation. It may be in the present tense (e.g. 'I sell this iPod to you for £100') or the past tense ('I sold this mobile to you for £50') but not in the form of an imperative (i.e. a command; e.g. 'sell me this book for £5!') or future tense (e.g. 'I'll sell this car to you next year for £1200') because the future tense does not denote certainty and contradicts a present intention and hence cannot be used to conclude a contract.[75]

- Offer and acceptance does not have to be in Arabic but can be in any language.
- Offer and acceptance is binding once both parties express it in agreement.
- Offer and acceptance can be established through other mechanisms such as written acceptance or indications (e.g. a nod or gesture).

The Conditions related to the Contractors (العاقد):

- Imām al-Kasānī writes:

أما الذي يرجع إلى العاقد فنوعان : أحدهما أن يكون عاقلا، فلا ينعقد بيع المجنون والصبي الذي لا يعقل... والثاني العدد في العاقد فلا يصلح الواحد عاقدا من الجانبين في باب البيع...

"As for the conditions that relate to the contractors, then they are two: (1) that the contractors have to be sane and discerning individuals so a mad person or an undiscerning child may not conduct a contract [...] and (2) the second

---

[75] al-Kasānī, *al-Badā'i` al-Ṣanā'i`*, 5:133-134.

condition i.e. the numbers of contractors hence there cannot be a person who undertakes a contract with himself..."[76]

The contractors:

[1] **Sane/rational/discerning persons (`*āqil*)**: a person must be in possession of a sound functioning intellect and not be mentally impaired, challenged or an undiscerning minor or child in order to undertake contractual actions.[77]

[2] **Two contractual parties (*al-`adad fī 'l-`āqid*)**: there must be two contractual parties present in order to exchange two counter-values.[78] This is because a contract where two values are being exchanged requires two representing parties to realise it. A contract may not be concluded by one legal proxy for both parties, nor can one sell something to himself and neither can he enter a contract with something fictional like an abstract entity.[79]

The General Conditions related to the Validity of <u>any</u> Contract (شرائط الصحة):

- Imām al-Kasānī writes:

وأما شرائط الصحة فأنواع : بعضها يعم البياعات كلها، وبعضها يخص البعض دون البعض أما الشرائط العامة فمنها : ما ذكرنا من شرائط الانعقاد والنفاذ ...ومنها أن يكون المبيع معلوما وثمنه معلوما علما يمنع من المنازعة ... ومنها : أن يكون مقدور التسليم من غير ضرر يلحق البائع فإن لم يمكن تسليمه إلا بضرر يلزمه فالبيع فاسد لأن الضرر لا يستحق بالعقد ولا يلزم بالتزام العاقد إلا ضرر تسليم المعقود عليه، فأما ما وراءه فلا... ومنها الخلو عن الشروط الفاسدة وهي أنواع . منها : شرط في وجوده غرر نحو ما إذا اشترى ناقة على

[76] al-Kasānī, *al-Badā'i` al-Ṣanā'i`*, 5:135-136.
[77] al-Kasānī, *al-Badā'i` al-Ṣanā'i`*, 5:134-136.
[78] al-Kasānī, *al-Badā'i` al-Ṣanā'i`*, 5:136.
[79] Except in the case of a father (*abb*), a legal guardian (*walī*) and a Judge (*qāḍī*).

أنها حامل ...ومنها شرط لا يقتضيه العقد وفيه منفعة للبائع أو للمشتري أو للمبيع إن كان من بني آدم كالرقيق وليس بملائم للعقد ولا مما جرى به التعامل بين الناس ...ومنها : شرط الأجل في المبيع العين والثمن العين وهو أن يضرب لتسليمها أجل ...ومنها : شرط خيار مؤبد في البيع ...ومنها : شرط خيار مؤقت بوقت مجهول جهالة متفاحشة كهبوب الريح ومجيء المطر وقدوم فلان وموت فلان ونحو ذلك أو متقاربة كالحصاد والدياس وقدوم الحاج ونحوها ... ومنها : شرط خيار غير مؤقت أصلا والأصل فيه أن شرط الخيار يمنع انعقاد العقد في حق الحكم للحال فكان شرطا مغيرا مقتضى العقد وإنه مفسد للعقد في الأصل وهو القياس إلا أنا عرفنا جوازه استحسانا بخلاف القياس بالنص ...ومنها شرط خيار مؤقت بالزائد على ثلاثة أيام عند أبي حنيفة وزفر ... ومنها الرضا لقول الله تعالى : إلا أن تكون تجارة عن تراض منكم ... ومنها القبض في بيع المشتري المنقول فلا يصح بيعه قبل القبض ...ومنها أن يكون البدل منطوقا به في أحد نوعي المبادلة، وهي المبادلة القولية فإن كان مسكوتا عنه فالبيع فاسد ...ومنها الخلو عن الربا ...

"As for the conditions related to the validity (*ṣiḥḥa*) of generally buying and selling, some are general for all contracts and some are specific to others. The more general conditions are: (1) the conditions related to undertaking and executing contracts that we have mentioned earlier […] (2) the item bought or sold must be known as well as its price so that disputes are eliminated […] (3) that the item bought or sold must be deliverable to the seller without harm otherwise the contract will be voidable […] (4) that the contract be free from any irregular elements and they are different such as: (4a) the element of *gharar* for example and other such uncertainties […] (4b) conditions that are not suitable or necessarily related to the contract that either benefits the buyer or the seller or the item being bought and sold […] (4c) that a condition is put delaying the item being bought […] (4d) that a condition is put that one has the option for perpetual trade […] (4e) that a condition is put for an option connected to designating a time but the time is unknown like when the 'when the blowing wind comes', or 'when the rain comes', 'or when so and so arrives or dies' […] (4f) that a condition is put that gives the option for an undesignated period of time […] (4g) that a condition is put that gives the option for exceeding three days according to Abū Ḥanīfa and

Zufar [...] (5) There must be approval from both parties based on the verse {***so that trade between you is based on mutual agreement***...} (6) there must be possession in deliverable goods as it is not valid to trade before there is any possession. […] (7) the exchange must be expressly stated according to one of the two types of exchanges which is verbal exchange so if one was silent during the contractual exchange, it would be voidable […] (8) and it must be free of *ribā*…"[80]

Conditions of general Validity:[81]

(1) Refer also to the pillar of the contract and the conditions of the contractors from above.

(2) **Ascertainment**: In buying and selling, the price and the item must be specified and known to both parties. Thus, one cannot offer an item for sale in vague terms, e.g. 'I'll sell you that mobile phone over there in that batch'. This is in order to eliminate *jahāla* (ignorance) in contractual negotiations, which is a means of removing disputes.[82]

(3) **Deliverability**: Any item being bought or sold must be deliverable to the other party. This means that the item must not in any way result in being damaged or destroyed upon its delivery. Thus, a contract will not be concluded until and unless the purchased item is delivered safely and securely. This also means the prohibition of selling any item whose delivery will result in the item itself being compromised, damaged or destroyed, e.g. stems of a plant, sleeves of a shirt, a brick from a wall, etc.[83]

(4a) **Uncertainty**: There should not be any uncertainties (*gharar*) within the contract whether related to the

---

[80] al-Kasānī, *al-Badā'i` al-Ṣanā'i`*, 5:168-193.
[81] This section follows the textual sequence of al-Kasānī's *al-Badā'i`*.
[82] al-Kasānī, *al-Badā'i` al-Ṣanā'i`*, 5:168f.
[83] al-Kasānī, *al-Badā'i` al-Ṣanā'i`*, 5:168-169.

object/item and price as this is a risk. This refers to intolerable degrees of *gharar* although some elements of uncertainty are tolerable and hence excused. Thus, for example, one cannot sell/buy something that one has no idea about, e.g. what is in the foetus of an animal.[84] This further relates to sales involving no idea of the consequence or outcome of the contract.[85]

(4c) **Delay**: An object being bought or sold must not be delayed or deferred. This is the normal requirement (*aṣl*) of a contract because a delay in delivering the bought item is contrary to immediate transfer of the item to the owner and will cause the contract to be voidable.[86] There should also be no delay or deferment in transferring the item to the buyer because there should be no hindrance in exchange of ownerships (i.e. the buyer owns the price and the seller owns the item) when it comes to objects of trade.[87]

(4d) **Perpetuity**: One must not put an option for perpetual trade (*mu'abbad*) as a condition for contractual negotiations, e.g. 'I'll sell this to you on the condition you keep it forever'.[88] In fact, no expiration period may be designated as a condition because ownership of a specific object/item does not have an expiration date.

(4e) **Future Contingent**: One cannot designate an incidental event, a contingent event or a mere future possibility as a condition of buying and selling. This is to eliminate extraneous uncertainties, e.g. one cannot negotiate a contract based on whether patterns, e.g. 'I'll sell this car to you if the wind blows easterly' or 'If it rains tonight, I'll sell this mobile to you for £100', etc.[89]

---

[84] al-Kasānī, *al-Badā'i` al-Ṣanā'i`*, 5:168-169.
[85] al-Kasānī, *al-Badā'i` al-Ṣanā'i`*, 5:169-170.
[86] al-Kasānī, *al-Badā'i` al-Ṣanā'i`*, 5:174.
[87] al-Kasānī, *al-Badā'i` al-Ṣanā'i`*, 5:174-175.
[88] al-Kasānī, *al-Badā'i` al-Ṣanā'i`*, 5:174.
[89] al-Kasānī, *al-Badā'i` al-Ṣanā'i`*, 5:174.

(4f) **Vagueness**: Any condition stipulated for a contract of buying and selling that is vague and unclear with regards to the period of time makes the contract voidable. This is because the unknown and undesignated time period is a means to possible confusion and dispute between the contracting parties (*nizā`*).[90]

(4g) **Three Days**: If exceeding three days is stipulated as an option in contractual negotiations, this will be voidable.[91]

(5) **Approval**: approval must exist in contractual negations and exchange of counter-values. Coercion and compulsion preclude approval and permission and hence make the contract voidable.[92]

(6) **Possession**: There must be possession (*qabḍ*) of the object of trade before any buying or selling takes place for the proper execution of the contract because it is not permitted generally to trade without actually possessing the merchandise, goods or objects.[93]

(7) **Clarity**: There must be express utterances or clear statements of contractual conditions in exchanges of counter-values. In other words, no contractual undertaking is permitted unless terms and conditions are made clear audibly or otherwise. Two contracting parties for example cannot make dealings and trade with each other without mentioning the details that are required, e.g. 'I've sold this wide-screen TV to you' – without mentioning the price – and the buyer states, 'Yeah, I accept that'. This is in order to eliminate uncertainty (*gharar*), ignorance (*jahāla*) and doubt that could be a cause for dispute later.[94]

---

[90] al-Kasānī, *al-Badā'i` al-Ṣanā'i`*, 5:174-175.
[91] al-Kasānī, *al-Badā'i` al-Ṣanā'i`*, 5:175-176.
[92] al-Kasānī, *al-Badā'i` al-Ṣanā'i`*, 5:176-177.
[93] al-Kasānī, *al-Badā'i` al-Ṣanā'i`*, 5:176-177.
[94] al-Kasānī, *al-Badā'i` al-Ṣanā'i`*, 5:182-183.

(8) ***Ribā***: Any contractual negotiation must avoid usurious elements, otherwise this will render the contract voidable.[95]

The Conditions related to the Subject Matter/Object of a Sale Contract (المعقود عليه):

- Imām al-Kasānī states:

وأما الذي يرجع إلى المعقود عليه فأنواع (منها) : أن يكون موجودا فلا ينعقد بيع المعدوم ... (ومنها) أن يكون مالا لأن البيع مبادلة المال بالمال، فلا ينعقد بيع الحر لأنه ليس بمال ... (ومنها) أن يكون مملوكا لأن البيع تمليك فلا ينعقد فيما ليس بمملوك كمن باع الكلأ في أرض مملوكة، والماء الذي في نهره أو في بئره ... (ومنها) وهو شرط انعقاد البيع للبائع أن يكون مملوكا للبائع عند البيع فإن لم يكن لا ينعقد ... (ومنها) أن يكون مقدور التسليم عند العقد، فإن كان معجوز التسليم عنده لا ينعقد ... (منها) أن يكون له مجيز عند وجوده فما لا مجيز له عند وجوده لا تلحقه الإجازة ... (ومنها) قيام المالك حتى لو هلك المالك قبل إجازته لا يجوز بإجازة ورثته . (ومنها) قيام المبيع حتى لو هلك قبل إجازة المالك لا يجوز بإجازة المالك غير أنه إن هلك في يد المالك يملك بغير شيء

"As for the subject matter [s: object] of a sale contract, its conditions are: (1) the item must be in existence because contracting on a non-existent item is ineffective [...] (2) it has to be a valid commodity (*mal*) recognized by the Law because trade is an exchange of commodities; hence it is not permitted to sell a free person as it is not a commodity [...] (3) The item must be owned because trade involves ownership and a contract cannot be effected if there is nothing to own [...] (4) that the owner must actually own the item at the time of the sale otherwise the sale will be ineffective [...] (5) It must be deliverable at the time of the contract otherwise the contract will be ineffective [...] (6) the owner must be alive throughout the contract conclusion such that if he were to die without giving his permission, his inheritors cannot automatically present permission on his behalf [...] (7) And the object of trade must be present

Climate health is a vital commodity.

---

[95] al-Kasānī, *al-Badā'i` al-Ṣanā'i`*, 5:182-183.

throughout the contract such that if it were to perish before the owner gives his permission it would not be valid..."[96]

The subject matter:

(1) **Existence of the object**: Whatever is traded must be in existence at the time and not non-existent because it is not permitted to sell or buy something that does not exist or is not tangible. **Examples**: selling the offspring of an offspring or selling fruits of a tree before they appear. Also, it is not permitted to trade in something that has the likelihood of ceasing to exist. **Examples**: sale of milk in the udder of a cow, selling an unborn animal in the mother's womb, etc.[97]

(2) **Deliverability**: Whatever is traded must be deliverable. Whatever is agreed with regards to the subject matter of a contract has to be deliverable at the time of concluding the contract. It is not permitted to trade in something that cannot in reality be delivered. **Examples**: a runaway slave or animal, birds in the air, random objects, etc.

(3) **Ascertainment**: Whatever is traded must be clearly ascertained and defined and should not be vague or incomprehensible. This refers to the price and description of the item of trade.

(4) **Ownership**: Whatever is traded must be actually owned by the respective party who are free to use it as they wish in the absence of legal constraints. If a third party has rights over the object of sale then the contract is suspended until it is properly clarified. **Examples**: a person cannot sell a house he is renting, etc. Related to this is the notion of private

---

[96] al-Kasānī, *al-Badā'i` al-Ṣanā'i`*, 5:138-151.

[97] Exceptions to this are: *bay` al-salam* (forward sale) and *bay` al-istiṣnā`* (manufacture contract with deferred payment) for which see al-Bashir, *Risk Management in Islamic Finance*, pp.49-61; Thomas et al, *Structuring Islamic Finance Transactions*, pp.93-101; Kettell, *Islamic Finance*, pp.74-80, 66-74 and Jamaldeen, *Islamic Finance*, pp.20-21.

property. Thus, public property may not be traded, e.g. grass for public grazing, water from a public canal or river, etc.

(5) **Legality**: Whatever is traded must be permitted by the Law. It is not permissible to trade in items that the Shariah prohibits. It is also not permitted to benefit from legally impermissible items. **Examples**: pork, alcohol, other religious objects, pornography, etc.

(6) **Life**: The owner must be alive as no contract negotiation or conclusion is permitted with the absence of the owner because h/her express permission is required. The death or loss of the owner does not entail that his prior permission immediately transfers to his inheritors.

(7) **Presence:** The object of trade/sale/exchange must be present through the duration of the contract so if it were to perish or be compromised before concluding the contract, then this would render the contract voidable. **Examples**: selling a house but it was demolished before contract was concluded; or selling a car but it was badly damaged before the contract could be concluded.

The Conditions related to the Place of a Contract (مكان العقد):

- Imām al-Kasānī comments:

وأما الذي يرجع إلى مكان العقد فواحد وهو اتحاد المجلس بأن كان الإيجاب والقبول في مجلس واحد، فإن اختلف المجلس لا ينعقد حتى لو أوجب أحدهما البيع فقام الآخر عن المجلس قبل القبول أو اشتغل بعمل آخر يوجب اختلاف المجلس ثم قبل لا ينعقد

"As for the matter that relates to the place or session of the contract, it is one condition which is the agreed place because the place where offer and acceptance is made is to be conducted in the same place. If there is disagreement over the place of the contract then the contract cannot be concluded such that if one were to give an offer of a sale and the other party got up and left the contractual place before accepting the offer or was busy with something else and then returned back to accept the [initial] offer, this will not be valid…"[98]

- Contracting while walking or driving is valid only if the offer and acceptance is agreed without any delay between them because delay will change the place (*majlis*) of the negotiation.[99]
- Contracting while on a ship, train or plane is valid whether moving or stationary because one has no control over these modes of transportation and so the journey would be considered one 'place' or 'session'.[100]
- Contracting with an absent party is not valid unless that absent party commissioned a legal proxy (representative) to act on their behalf.[101]
- Contracting via written communication (letter, email, fax, etc.) is valid so long as upon receipt of the written communication, the offer/acceptance is accepted.[102]

The Conditions related to Contractual Options (الخيار):

The default in a contract is that it is binding, as the contract is the medium for an exchange of ownership to take place. However, there are certain 'options' (*khiyār*) permitted by the Shariah to service the needs of the contractual parties.[103] These options exist to manage a number of hindrances to contracts such as:

---

[98] al-Kasānī, *al-Badā'i` al-Ṣanā'i`*, 5:136-137.
[99] Ibn al-Humām, *Fatḥ al-Qadīr*, 5:79.
[100] Ibn al-Humām, *Fatḥ al-Qadīr*, 5:79.
[101] Ibn al-Humām, *Fatḥ al-Qadīr*, 5:79-80.
[102] Ibn al-Humām, *Fatḥ al-Qadīr*, 5:80.
[103] Kharofa, *Transactions in Islamic Law*, p.92.

1. Fraud.
2. Misrepresentation.
3. Default risk.
4. Ownership risk.
5. Market risk.
6. Price risk.

The key options include:

- *Khiyār al-majlis*: Each party is permitted to cancel or confirm a contract in a particular contractual session, place or meeting (*majlis*) that requires it.[104]

- *Khiyār al-sharṭ*: Each party has in some instances the option to either confirm or cancel a sale within a set period of time, either agreed by the parties or according to some no more than three days.[105]

- *Khiyār al-ru'ya*: the right of the purchaser to cancel or confirm a sale based on the option to inspect the goods under consideration.[106]

- *Khiyār al-`ayb*: When a party has the right to cancel or confirm a sale based on the deficiencies and defects in a particular item or good such that it fails to meet the agreed expectations and standards of the contract.[107]

- *Khiyār al-ghubn*: Each party has the right to revoke a contract or cancel it based on deception, fraud, misrepresentations and lies.[108]

[104] Ibid., pp.92-97.
[105] Ibid., pp.98-109.
[106] Ibid., pp.110-117.
[107] Ibid., pp.118-142.
[108] al-Zuḥaylī, *Financial Transactions*, 1:172-174.

Thus, these various options allow for the contractual parties to:

[1] Time to ponder over the value, worth, need and viability of a particular contract.

[2] Offer time to reduce damage and risk to both contractual parties in case of hastiness in undertaking the conclusion of the contract.[109]

The Conditions related to dissolution of a Contract:

Contractual parties have the right to dissolve (*faskh*) a contract based on the following general causes:

1. Death of one of the contractual parties.

2. If one of the contractual parties was forced or coerced.

3. Failure of a contractual commitment from one of the contractual parties, e.g. non-payment for the goods bought, etc.

4. Deceit, fraud or cheating.

[109] M. B. Arbouna, "Option Contracts and the Principle of Sale of Rights in Sharī`ah" in *Islamic Banking and Finance: Fundamentals and Contemporary Issues*, ed. by S. S. Ali and A. Ahmed, pp.51-80.

Invalid Types *of* Contracts

Invalid Types of Contracts:

1. Related to the Contractors

2. Related to the Subject-matter of the Contract

3. Related to the *Ribā*

4. Related to the *Gharar*

5. Other invalid Contract Types

Chapter 5: *Invalid Types of Contracts*

♦

In this Chapter:

- Outlines.
- Related to the Contractors.
- Related to the Subject-matter/object of the Contract.
- Related to the *Ribā*.
- Related to the *Gharar*.
- Other invalid Contract types.

Outline:

There are many types of contracts that Shariah does not consider valid discussed by Muslim scholars. Below is a list of common contract types with examples that do not conform to Shariah stipulations treated in the *fiqh* books and hence cannot be executed (although there are noted scholarly differences regarding some). The list is categorised according to a related area of the contract that renders it invalid. Capital letters like A, B, C, etc. stand for contracting parties (person, banks, companies, institutions, etc) and the symbol *x* stands for some asset (commodity, item of trade).

Related to the Contractors:

- بيع المكره : A sells *x* to B where B is coerced to purchase *x*, e.g. A says to B, 'You will buy this car or I will put you in hospital!' This is an invalid type because contracts must be concluded with agreement and consent of both parties. The same holds for scenarios of compulsion, abuse, torture, extreme threat to life, or severe blackmail.

- بيع المجنون : A sells *x* to B where B is insane, mentally ill or unfit to dispose of his own affairs, e.g. A offers a mobile contract to B who is a mentally unfit person obtaining some form of approval from him. Such a contract is void due to *non compos mentis*, i.e. B lacks the *capacity* to correctly administer a contract.

- بيع الأعمى : A sells *x* to B who is blind, e.g. A is an online company that has sales on technical items like a laptop and B is a customer who has complete visual impairment wants to purchase an item from this online sale. Some scholars have considered this impermissible because B does not have the capacity to inspect the goods in order to make an informed decision for purchase. However, other scholars have considered the contract valid if the product is described accurately and with relevant detail.

- بيع الفضولي : A buys *x* for B but was not given authority to purchase *x*, e.g. A is an agent for B and comes across a great deal thinking that B would like it and so purchases *x* on his behalf with B's money. Such a contract, a form of *negotium gestor*, is void due to it being officious and unauthorised by B. If however, B gives his belated consent or approval, then the contract would be valid and concluded.

- بيع الصبي : A sells to B where B is a minor or child, e.g. a boy walks into a toyshop and buys a toy and the customer assistance processes the transaction. Some scholars have prohibited this kind of sale whereas Imām Abū Ḥanīfa and others permitted it pending approval of the guardian of the legal guardian if the child is discerning (*mumayyiz*).[110]

---

[110] al-Nawawī in *al-Majmū`*, 9:185 states the different positions:

- بيع المحجور عليه : A is under interdiction (deprived of disposing his own affairs) due to mental incapacity, illness, or legal restraint such as squandering or being unfit financially. Contracts pertaining to A with another person B are pending approval from whoever is the legally appointed guardian of A.

- A sells x to B but B did not give his official approval. B's consent was forged by someone else, e.g. A is an online company selling video games and B is an online customer. Some other person C uses B's credit card to purchase x from the internet without his consent. Such a contract is a type of *non est factum* where B denies any involvement in the contract done in his name. This is strictly forbidden in Shariah and a major sin as it involves stealing, fraud and deception.

Related to the Subject-matter/object of the Contract:

- بيع المعدوم : A sells x to B but x does not exist. This violates a condition of the contract, which is that the object of the sale must be in existence.

- بيع معجوز التسليم : A sells x to B where x is something that cannot be delivered, e.g. birds in the sky, a fish in the sea, etc. This contravenes a condition of the

---

مبينا مذاهب العلماء في ذلك: " فرع في مذاهب العلماء في بيع الصبي المميز: قد ذكرنا أن مذهبنا أنه لا يصح سواء أذن له الولي أم لا وبه قال أبو ثور. وقال الثوري وأبو حنيفة وأحمد وإسحاق: يصح بيعه وشراؤه بإذن وليه . وعن أبي حنيفة رواية أنه يجوز بغير إذنه ويقف على إجازة الولي , قال ابن المنذر : وأجاز أحمد وإسحاق بيعه وشراءه في الشيء اليسير يعني بلا إذن" ...

Ibn Qudāma in *al-Mughnī*, 4:168 states:

ويصح تصرف الصبي المميز بالبيع والشراء فيما أذن له الولي فيه ، في إحدى الروايتين . وهو قول أبي حنيفة

contract, which is that an item of sale must be deliverable.

- بيع النجس والمتنجس : A sells x to B where x is something the Shariah considers impure (*najis*) like flesh, carrion, blood, pork, wine, dust, etc. This is strictly prohibited and cannot be undertaken in any way. Many scholars extend this to include goods that are spoiled or tainted (*mutanajjas*), e.g. oil, honey, butter that have rodents or other living animals fallen inside it.

Related to the *Ribā*:

- A (creditor) loans £10,000 (principle) to B (debtor) for 5 years with a return of £15,000 over that period. This is prohibited because it is an unwarranted surplus of £5000 on the principle.
- A loans B £10,000 to be repaid in full by January 2010 but increases the amount to £12,000 if B defers to another month, say February. This is prohibited because it is an unwarranted demand for surplus on the loaned principle simply because of a delay in time.

Related to the *Gharar*:

There are a number of areas that scholars argue *gharar* applies to such as:

1. **(تعذر التسليم):** items that cannot be delivered in reality, e.g. a runaway slave, etc.
2. **(الجهل بجنس الثمن أو المثمون):** selling something whose price or object of sale is not known, e.g. 'I'll sell you

what's beyond that wall,' or 'I'll sell you whatever is in my bag', etc. what is beyond the wall or in the bag is utterly undefined, vague and unspecified.

3. (الجهل بصفة الثمن أو المثمون): selling something the description or quality the seller does not know, e.g. 'I'll sell one of those shirts in my store', 'I'll sell you one of the dresses that I have on my stall', etc. where the shirt or dress quality is not defined by the seller.[111]

4. (الجهل بمقدار المبيع أو الثمن): Selling something whose quantity or price is not specified, e.g. 'I'll buy this at today's price', or 'I'll buy at whatever price and whatever quantity', etc. because these are vague terms of a deal – what price and what quantity is meant or intended by the buyer is not clear.

5. (الجهل بالأجل): selling something with a vague term of deferment, e.g. 'I'll sell you this cooker when my manager comes back from holiday', or 'I'll buy this when it gets warmer', etc. all of which are unclear and unspecified times.

6. (بيعتان في بيعة): 'two sales in one', i.e. when something is sold for two prices, e.g. 'I'll sell you this shirt for £10 now in cash or pay later for £20.' This kind of sale is not valid. Choice of one of the price offers would however conclude the sale.

7. (بيع ما لا ترجى سلامته): selling something whose good status that is not expected, e.g. a sick horse.

8. (بيع الحصى): a pre-Islamic form of sale known as a 'pebble throw sale' where the seller carries a pebble in his hand or tosses a pebble in the air and whatever

[111] It is, however, permissible to buy in bulk, i.e. wholesale quantities.

that pebble lands on, the buyer had to buy that item.[112]

9. (بيع المنابذة): a pre-Islamic mode of exchange known as a 'throw sale' where two traders would literally toss each other items of clothing without inspecting it.[113]

10. (بيع الملامسة): a pre-Islamic mode of sale known as a 'touch sale' where whatever item the buyer happened to touch, he had to buy that even if he did not inspect it.[114]

Other invalid Contract Types:

- بيع العربون: A sells *x* to B where B offers a down payment (or an advance payment) to secure *x* as part of the price but if B were to later change his mind, A would retain the down payment figure, e.g. A sells a car to B and agrees a deposit (= down payment/advance payment) figure of £100 with B. If B pays £100 to secure the car and proceeds to buy it, the £100 goes towards the overall price but if B later withdraws from the sale, then A is entitled to keep the £100. This is known as the *`arbūn* sale. Most scholars do not permit this kind of sale based on a narration from the Prophet whereas others permitted it disputing the validity of the narrations.[115]

---

[112] Hassan, *Sales and Contract*, pp.50-51.
[113] Ibid., p.52.
[114] Ibid., pp.51-52. For other pre-Islamic contract types, see pp.47-75.
[115] The Fiqh Council Resolution No. 72 (3/8) 1993, no. 8, 1:641 declares this type of sale as permissible:

1. المراد ببيع السلعة مع دفع المشتري مبلغاً من المال إلى البائع على أنه إن أخذ السلعة احتسب المبلغ من الثمن وإن تركها فالمبلغ للبائع. ويجري مجرى البيع الإجارة، لأنها بيع المنافع. ويستثنى من البيوع كل ما يشترط لصحته قبض أحد البدلين في مجلس العقد (السلم) أو قبض

- بيع العينة : A sells *x* to B for a deferred payment but then buys back *x* from B immediately for a lesser price, e.g. A sells a car to B for £5,000 (= purchase price [£4,000] + profit [£1,000]) to be paid for by B in 6 months (July) or in instalments over 6 months. B sells the car back to A for £4,000 (purchase price) thus in effect gaining £1,000 and will agree to pay A £5,000 in July, 6 months after. Thus, a form of a swap takes place where one party gains instant cash or some compensation over the other creating a kind of loan in the form of a sale. This is known as the *`īna* contract. Many scholars have evaluated this as a disguised *ribā* contract.[116]

- بيع التصريف : A sells *x* to B but B stipulates the condition that A take back whatever B was unable to sell of *x* but B will pay the price for whatever he was able to sell of *x*, e.g. B buys shirts wholesale from A and agrees with A to return any unsold shirts back but will pay for whatever shirts he was able to sell. This is known as the 'Taṣrīf' contract and is not permitted by majority of the scholars because it involves extreme uncertainty and ignorance over the outcome

---

البدلين (مبادلة الأموال الربوية والصرف) ولا يجري في المرابحة للآمر بالشراء في مرحلة المواعدة ولكن يجري في مرحلة البيع التالية للمواعدة.

2. يجوز بيع العربون إذا قيدت فترة الانتظار بزمن محدود. ويحتسب العربون جزءاً من الثمن إذا تم الشراء، ويكون من حق البائع إذا عدل المشتري عن الشراء.

[116] Abū Ḥanīfa did not permit it based on a *ḥadīth* whereas Abū Yūsuf did permit it. Ibn al-Humām quotes al-Ḥasan al-Shaybānī as expressing dislike for it:

"This kind of transaction weighs heavy like mountains on my heart. It was invented by those who consume *ribā*…" See *Fatḥ al-Qadīr*, 7:213:

هذا البيع في قلبي كأمثال الجبال، اخترعه أَكَلَةُ الربا

of the sale in that the seller does not know how many items will be returned and the seller does not know how much will be bought. Thus, to stipulate this as a condition would render the contract either void or invalid.[117]

- بيع التقسيط : A sells x to B on instalment but for an increased price, e.g. A sells to B a new car for £10,000 over 12 months (1 year) with an increment of 1% per month (= 12%/£1200 for that year totalling £12,000). If A considers the 1% increment separately from the contract then this is unlawful as it is tantamount to an unwarranted excess or surplus on the original price. However, if A figured the increment as part of his profit margin on the car and factored that in the overall price, then that would be permitted, e.g. A sold the car to B for £12,000 over 12 months where the figure '£12,000' incorporates his calculation of the overall profit. This is the 'Taqsīt' contract. Some scholars disapprove of this kind of sale but it is generally deemed valid.[118]

---

[117] Ibn Qudāma, *al-Mughnī*, 4:286:

ففيه وجهان (أحدهما) يجبر لأن شرط العتق إذا صح تعلق بعينه فيجبر عليه كما لو نذر عتقه (والثاني) لا يجبر لأن الشرط لا يوجب فعل المشروط بدليل ما لو شرط الرهن والضمين، فعلى هذا يثبت للبائع خيار الفسخ لأنه لم يسلم له ما شرطه له أشبه ما لو شرط عليه رهنا، وان تعب المبيع أو كان أمة فأحبلها أعتقه وأجزأه لأن الرق باق فيه، وإن استغله أو أخذ من كسبه شيئا فهو له، وإن مات المبيع رجع البائع على المشتري بما نقصه شرط العتق فيقال كم قيمته لو بيع مطلقا، وكم يساوي إذا بيع بشرط العتق؟ فيرجع بقسط ذلك من ثمنه في أحد الوجهين وفي الآخر يضمن ما نقص من قيمته (الضرب الثاني) أن يشترط غير العتق مثل أن يشترط أن لا يبيع ولا يهب ولا يعتق ولا يطأ أو يشترط عليه أن يبيعه أو يقفه أو متى نفق المبيع وإلا رده، أو إن غصبه غاصب رجع عليه بالثمن، وان أعتقه فالولاء له فهذه وما أشبهها شروط فاسدة وهل يفسد بها البيع؟ على روايتين. قال القاضي المنصوص عن أحمد ان البيع صحيح وهو ظاهر كلام الخرقي ههنا وهو قول الحسن والشعبي والنخعي والحكم وابن أبي ليلى وأبي ثور (والثانية) البيع فاسد وهو مذهب أبو حنيفة والشافعي لأن النبي صلى الله عليه وسلم نهى عن بيع وشرط ولأنه شرط فاسد فأفسد البيع

[118] See the Fiqh Academy Resolution 51 (6/2), 1990, 1:93 (no.6) and 2:9 (no.7) on this type of contract:

- بيع الشيء قبل القبض : A sells x to B but had not gained possession of x, i.e. x was neither in his physical custody (e.g. in his hand) nor in his capacity to access and control it (e.g. he has access to it but it is not in his physical custody). This is generally held to be invalid because one of the conditions is the seller must have possession – whether actual or constructive – of the goods he is selling.

- البيع وقت النداء لصلاة الجمعة : This is considered to be trade on Friday during the time the Imam ascends to the *minbar* (platform) to deliver the Friday sermon or when the first of the two calls to the prayer (*adhān*) is made. Many scholars consider any trade at this time prohibited and some invalid from its inception.

- بيع العنب لعاصر الخمر : A sells grapes to B knowing full well that B is a winemaker. This type of sale extends to all types of direct assistance in sin, e.g. selling a weapon to someone intending to kill someone else, or trading with a company that is only involved in unlawful activities or unlawful items of trade.[119]

- بيع الإنسان على بيع أخيه : A arranges a contract to sell a house to B for £200,000 and arranges an appointment for B through his estate agent for an inspection of the house. Another person C then proposes to A an offer of £250,000 instead if A voids his sale with B and

---

لا يجوز شرعا في بيع الأجل التنصيص في العقد على فوائد التقسيط مفصولة عن الثمن الحالي بحيث ترتبط بالأجل سواء اتفق المتعاقدان على نسبة الفائدة أم ربطاها بالفائدة السائدة

119 See K. al-Jabalī, "I`āna `alā 'l-Ma`ṣiya fī 'l-Mu`āmalāt al-Māliyya", *Journal of the Islamic University*, no. 155, pp.359-404 and Mufti Shafi's *Tafṣīl al-Kalām fī Mas'alat al-I`āna `alā 'l-Ḥarām*. See also §. 'Jobs that directly assist and lead to Sin' in my *Introducing the Fiqh of Employment* based on Mufti Shafi's *Tafṣīl al-Kalām*.

promises that he will honour that. Scholars consider this kind of undercutting and interjection as impermissible based on the Prophet prohibiting the sabotage of an existing contract of sale.[120]

- بيع النجش : A is selling *x* to customers and B (in collusion with A) comes along and bargains for it and offers a very high price without any intention to actually purchase. He only seeks to create a hike in the price of *x* in order to make customers pay more. This kind of sale is condemned by all scholars as being fraudulent.[121]

- بيع المزايدة : This is the auction sale (al-*muzāyada*) where in a particular gathering, items are sold to the highest bidder. Some scholars have forbidden this kind of sale although majority of the scholars have permitted it based on the Prophet's explicit action of engaging in an auction.[122]

---

[120] al-Shawkānī, *Nayl al-Awṭār*, 5:167: **"Let none of you supplant the sale of his brother"**:

لا يبع أحدكم على بيع أخيه

[121] The Ḥanafī scholars rule the sale is valid but those who collude in this way are sinful for doing so. However, if the price is neither exaggerated nor raised excessively, then there is no sin in this. Kharofa, *Transactions in Islamic Law*, pp.89-90.

[122] Tirmidhī, *Sunan* (#1139):

أَنَسِ بْنِ مَالِكٍ أَنَّ رَسُولَ اللَّهِ صَلَّى اللَّهُ عَلَيْهِ وَسَلَّمَ بَاعَ حِلْسًا (بساط للأرض أو كساء لظهر الدابة) وَقَدَحًا وَقَالَ مَنْ يَشْتَرِي هَذَا الْحِلْسَ وَالْقَدَحَ فَقَالَ رَجُلٌ أَخَذْتُهُمَا بِدِرْهَمٍ فَقَالَ النَّبِيُّ صَلَّى اللَّهُ عَلَيْهِ وَسَلَّمَ مَنْ يَزِيدُ عَلَى دِرْهَمٍ مَنْ يَزِيدُ عَلَى دِرْهَمٍ فَأَعْطَاهُ رَجُلٌ دِرْهَمَيْنِ فَبَاعَهُمَا مِنْهُ

"From Anas b. Mālik who said that the Messenger of Allah sold a rug (for spreading on the ground or putting on the back of a riding-beast) and a cup. He asked: **'Who will buy this rug and cup?'** A man replied: 'I'll take them for a dirham,' and the Prophet said: **'Who will offer more than a dirham? Who will offer more than a dirham?'** Another man gave him two dirhams and bought the goods…"

- بيع وشرط : A sells *x* to B on the condition that B is not allowed to sell *x* to C. This is known as a 'sale with an invalid condition' (*bay` wa sharṭ*. These kinds of conditional sales bring about harm or loss to one of the parties with that unwarranted condition. Most scholars hold the sale to be valid in such a case and dismiss the condition as legally ineffective. If positive conditions are stipulated (that brings about a benefit to one of the parties), then this is acceptable for some scholars, e.g. A says to B, 'I'll buy this laptop if you can deliver it to my house.'

- الجمع في صفقة واحدة بين البيع وبين أحد ستة عقود : A enters into a contract with B but stipulates an additional contract from one of the following six categories:

[1] promise (الجعالة);
[2] currency exchange (الصرف);
[3] sharecropping (المساقاة);
[4] partnership (الشركة);
[5] marriage (النكاح) and
[6] Passive partnership (المضاربة), e.g. 'I'll sell you *x* on the condition that you let me marry your sister', or 'I'll buy *x* on the condition that you also be my partner in a new business', or 'I'll buy that car off you if you promise to sell me your motorbike', etc.

Conventional Insurance Contracts

Conventional Insurance Contracts:

1. Insurance contracts
2. Warranties and Extended Warranty contracts

Chapter 6

♦

Insurance (التأمين) and Extended Warranties

In this section

- What conventional insurance involves.
- Common insurance contracts.
- The Islamic viewpoint regarding conventional insurance policies.
- Additional Rulings.

Conventional Insurance:

> Definition: A contract (policy) in which an individual or entity receives financial protection or reimbursement against losses from an insurance company. The company pools clients' risks to make payments more affordable for the insured.[123]

An insurance policy involves a contract between the insured (*policyholder*) and the insurer that lays out the claims the insurer is legally required to pay in the event of some loss or damage. The basic underlying concept of an insurance contract is:

A (insurer) promises to pay B (insured) for future uncertain losses and damages that are covered according to an agreed policy language and document with terms/conditions in exchange for payments (*premium*).

---

[123] s.v. "Insurance" at http://www.investopedia.com/terms/i/insurance.asp

Common insurance policies cover the following areas:

1. Health.
2. Travel.
3. Fire.
4. Life.
5. Property.
6. Pets.
7. Home.
8. Social.
9. Liability.
10. Items (mobiles, laptops, etc.).

Example: Policyholder B pays insurance company A monthly amounts of £100 for *coverage* (protection) over some future uncertain event such as loss, peril, danger or accident (e.g. property damage, personal accident, health, etc.). Upon the loss, peril, danger or accident occurring say in month 6 (June), A would be bound to pay the benefits to B more than or less than the original premium figure (£600). Thus, A is compensating B for an uncertainty.

Islamic viewpoint:[124]

---

[124] Discussed by Mufti Taqi Usmani, *Islam Aur Jadīd Ma'īshat*, pp.159-163; Zuḥaylī, *Financial Transactions*, 1:87-97, Nyazee, Islamic Law of Contract, pp.379-404 and Visser, *Islamic Finance: Principles and Practice*, pp.128-134. For various stances by contemporary religious figures on conventional insurance, see for example Sh. `Aṭā' b. Khalīl, "Regarding Health Insurance" available at http://www.hizb-ut-tahrir.info/info/english.php/contents_en/entry_29848; Idem, "About Subscribing to Social Insurance" available at http://www.hizb-ut-tahrir.info/info/english.php/contents_en/entry_31207; Sh. Suhaib Webb, "Fatwa on Life Insurance" available at http://www.suhaibwebb.com who argues for its need based on "social necessity"; M. Kahf, "Fatwa on Insurance" available at http://monzer.kahf.com; Mufti I. Haq, "Car Insurance, Home Insurance, Health Insurance..." available at http://www.askamufti.com/ Sh. Ṣāliḥ al-Munajjid, "The true nature of

Islamically, an insurance contract of this nature is strictly prohibited for the following reasons:

[1] *Qimār* (gambling): It may or may not be the case that the insurance company pays out more than the initial premium paid by the insured for coverage of some loss or damage. This in the Shariah is tantamount to gambling. Thus, if B pays A £100 over a period of 6 months (= £600) and makes a claim for some adverse event occurring in the seventh month, it is possible that B receives more than the initial premium he paid or less (> £600 or < £600). This possibility of more or less than with respect to B, is tantamount to gambling.

[2] *Ribā* (usury): If the insurance company receives premiums worth more than the value of what is insured, then that will be tantamount to an interest/usury exchange. If there is any loss on what is insured and the loss is worth less than the total premium paid to the insurance company, such a person would be guilty of undertaking a usurious and interest based transaction as in either case, there is an unwarranted excess or gain on wealth.

[3] *Gharar* (future uncertainty): the insurance company is obligated to adhere to the terms of the insurance policy if a future uncertain event did occur. Being bound to compensate financially for an unspecified, random and uncertain event (i.e. a future contingency) is not permitted in Shariah due to the clear textual prohibition on this.[125] The insurance

---

insurance and the rulings concerning it" available at http://islamqa.info/en/8889; Mufti Ibn Adam al-Kawthari, "Car Insurance Issues" available at http://spa.qibla.com and Mufti I. Ibn Moosa, "Insurance Policy…" available at http://www.askimam.org.

[125] Ibn `Ābidīn, *Radd al-Muḥtār*, 4:350:

مطلب مهم فيما يفعله التجار من دفع ما يسمى سوكرة وتضمين الحربي ما هلك في المركب وبما قررناه يظهر جواب ما كثر السؤال عنه في زماننا: وهو أنه جرت العادة أن التجار إذا استأجروا مركبا من حربي يدفعون له أجرته، ويدفعون أيضا مالا معلوما لرجل حربي مقيم في بلاده، يسمى ذلك المال: سوكرة، على أنه مهما هلك

company does not know the extent of the compensation nor if there will even be one.[126]

A *Fatwā* on Marine Insurance:

Ibn `Ābidīn issued a *fatwā* on marine insurance and argued for its impermissibility on a number of grounds. Below is the Arabic text followed by al-Zuḥaylī's explanation of it with his short summary:[127]

Ibn `Ābidīn:

مطلب مهم فيما يفعله التجار من دفع ما يسمى سوكرة وتضمين الحربي ما هلك في المركب وبما قررناه يظهر جواب ما كثر السؤال عنه في زماننا: وهو أنه جرت العادة أن التجار إذا استأجروا مركبا من حربي يدفعون له أجرته، ويدفعون أيضا مالا معلوما لرجل حربي مقيم في بلاده، يسمى ذلك المال: سوكرة، على أنه مهما هلك من المال الذي في المركب بحرق أو غرق أو نهب أو غيره، فذلك الرجل ضامن له بمقابلة ما يأخذه منهم، وله وكيل عنه مستأمن في دارنا، يقيم في بلاد السواحل الاسلامية بإذن السلطان، يقبض من التجار مال السوكرة،

من المال الذي في المركب بحرق أو غرق أو نهب أو غيره، فذلك الرجل ضامن له بمقابلة ما يأخذه منهم، وله وكيل عنه مستأمن في دارنا، يقيم في بلاد السواحل الاسلامية بإذن السلطان، يقبض من التجار مال السوكرة، وإذا هلك من مالهم في البحر شئ يؤدي ذلك المستأمن للتجار بدله تماما، والذي يظهر لي: أنه لا يحل للتاجر أخذ بدل الهالك من ماله، لان هذا التزام ما لا يلزم.

[126] See The Islamic Fiqh Academy, Resolution No. 9 (9/2) on the categorical prohibition of insurance, 2:545 based on intolerable *gharar*:

أولاً: أن عقد التأمين التجاري ذي القسط الثابت الذي تتعامل به شركات التأمين التجاري عقد فيه غرر كبير مفسد للعقد. ولذا فهو حرام شرعاً.

See also S. Nu Nu Htay et al, *Accounting, Auditing and Governance for Takaful Operations*, pp.5-7 and the research paper by Mufti M. Z. Butt, "Breakdown Cover – A Discussion" available at http://alqalam.org.uk

[127] See *Radd al-Muḥtār*, 4:250-251 and al-Zuḥaylī, *al-Fiqh al-Islāmī*, 5:103.

وإذا هلك من مالهم في البحر شئ يؤدي ذلك المستأمن للتجار بدله تماما، والذي يظهر لي: أنه لا يحل للتاجر أخذ بدل الهالك من ماله، لان هذا التزام ما لا يلزم.

فإن قلت: إن المودع إذا أخذ أجرة على الوديعة يضمنها إذا هلكت. قلت: ليست مسألتنا من هذا القبيل، لان المال ليس في يد صاحب السوكرة، بل في يد صاحب المركب، وإن كان صاحب السوكرة هو صاحب المركب يكون أجيرا مشتركا قد أخذ أجرة على الحفظ وعلى الحمل، وكل من المودع والأجير المشترك لا يضمن ما لا يمكن الاحتراز عنه كالموت والغرق ونحو ذلك .

فإن قلت: سيأتي قبيل باب كفالة الرجلين قال لآخر: اسلك هذا الطريق فإنه آمن، فسلك وأخذ ماله لم يضمن، ولو قال: إن كان مخوفا وأخذ مالك فأنا ضامن: ضمن، وعلله الشارح هناك بأنه ضمن الغار صفة السلامة للمغرور نصا اه: أي بخلاف الأولى، فإنه لم ينص على الضمان بقوله: فأنا ضامن، وفي جامع الفصولين: الأصل أن المغرور إنما يرجع على الغار لو حصل الغرور في ضمن المعاوضة، أو ضمن الغار صفة السلامة للمغرور فيصار كقول الطحان لرب البر:جعله في الدلو فجعله فيه، فذهب من النقب إلى الماء، وكان الطحان عالما به يضمن، إذ غره في ضمن العقد وهو يقتضي السلامة اه.

قلت: لا بد في مسألة التغرير من أن يكون الغار عالما بالخطر كما يدل عليه مسألة الطحان المذكورة وأن يكون المغرور غير عالم، إذ لا شك أن رب البر لو كان عالما بنقب الدلو يكون هو المضيع لما له باختياره، ولفظ المغرور ينبئ عن ذلك لغة لما في القاموس: غيره غرا وغرورا فهو مغرور وغرير: خدعه وأطمعه بالباطل فاغتر هو اه. ولا يخفى أن صاحب السوكرة لا يقصد تغرير التجار، ولا يعلم بحصول الغرق هل يكون أم لا. وأما الخطر من اللصوص والقطاع فهو معلوم له وللتجار، لأنهم لا يعطون مال السوكرة عند شدة الخوف طمعا في أخذ بدل الهالك، فلم تكن مسألتنا من هذا القبيل أيضا، نعم: قد يكون للتاجر شريك حربي في بلاد الحرب، فيعقد شريكه هذا العقد مع صاحب السوكرة في بلادهم، ويأخذ منه بدل الهالك ويرسله إلى التاجر، فالظاهر أ هذا يحل للتاجر أخذه لأن العقد الفاسد جرى بين حربيين في بلاد الحرب، وقد وصل إليه مالهم برضاهم فلا مانع من أخذه، وقد يكون التاجر في بلادهم، فيعقد معهم هناك، ويقبض البدل في بلادنا أو بالعكس، ولا شك أنه في الأولى إن حصل بينهما خصام في بلادنا لا نقضي للتاجر بالبدل، وإن لم

يحصل خصام ودفع له البدل وكيله المستأمن هنا يحل له أخذه، لأن العقد الذي صار في بلادهم لا حكم له، فيكون قد أخذ مال حربي برضاه. وأما في صورة العكس، بأن كان العقد في بلادنا والقبض في بلادهم، فالظاهر أنه لا يحل أخذه، ولو برضا الحربي لابتنائه على العقد الفاسد الصادر في بلاد الاسلام، فيعتبر حكمه، هذا ما ظهر لي في تحرير هذه المسألة فاغتنمه فإنه لا تجده في غير هذا الكتاب

al-Zuḥaylī's comments:

فتوى ابن عابدين: أفتى ابن عابدين بحرمة التأمين البحري، لضمان ما قد يهلك من البضائع المستوردة بطريق النقل البحري، بالمراكب، فلا يحل للتاجر أخذ بدل الهالك من مال المؤمِّن لأسباب ثلاثة:

١ – إن هذا العقد التزام ما لا يلزم، لعدم وجود سبب شرعي من أسباب الضمان الأربعة وهي العدوان من قتل وهدم وإحراق ونحوها، وتسبب الإتلاف كحفر بئر بدون ترخيص في الطريق العام، ووضع اليد غير المؤتمنة كالغصب والسرقة وبقاء المبيع في يد البائع، والكفالة. وليس المؤمِّن متعدياً، ولا متسبباً في الإتلاف، ولا واضع يد على المؤمن عليه، وليس في التأمين مكفول معين.

٢ – ليس التأمين من قبيل تضمين الوديع إذا أخذ أجراً على الوديعة إذا هلكت: لأن المال ليس في يد المؤمن، بل في يد صاحب المركب، ولو كان صاحب المركب هو المؤمن، فإنه يكون أجيراً مشتركاً، لا وديعاً، وكل من الوديع والأجير المشترك لا يضمن ما لا يمكن الاحتراز عنه، كالموت والغرق والحرق الغالب.

٣ – ليس التأمين من قبيل تضمين التغرير: لأن الغارّ لا بد من أن يكون عالماً بالخطر، وأن يكون المغرور جاهلاً به غير عالم. والمؤمن (شركة التأمين أو الضمان) لا يقصد تغرير التجار (المؤمن لهم)، ولا يعلم بحصول الخطر . الغرق مثلاً . هل يكون أو لا، أي لا يعلم: هل تغرق المركب أو لا؟ أما في حال العلم بالخطر من المؤمن والتاجر كالخطر من اللصوص قطاع الطرق، فيجوز الضمان، ولكن ليس التأمين منطبقاً عليها. فلو قال شخص لآخر: اسلك هذا الطريق، فإن كان مخوفاً وأخذ مالك، فأنا ضامن : ضمن.

Other objections include:

- Insurance is a form of *ghubn* (fraud) because the subject of the contract is not known.
- Insurance contracts involve high levels of *jahāla* (ignorance) as neither party knows the extent or scope of either loss or profit.

Additional Rulings:

- If a country makes insurance legislatively mandatory, then the payment of insurance some scholars say is permissible because insurance would then be a necessity for a person to obtain their lawful right to drive. Whatever insurance arrangement or policy minimally enables the right to be obtained must be paid, e.g. third party vehicle insurance and not comprehensive cover.[128]

- If insurance of some kind is already contained within a contract (e.g. travel insurance within a holiday

---

[128] Ibn `Ābidīn, *Radd al-Muḥtār*, 5:362:

الرَّابِعُ: مَا يَدْفَعُ لِدَفْعِ الْخَوْفِ مِنْ الْمَدْفُوعِ إلَيْهِ عَلَى نَفْسِهِ أَوْ مَالِهِ حَلَالٌ لِلدَّافِعِ حَرَامٌ عَلَى الْآخِذِ؛ لِأَنَّ دَفْعَ الضَّرَرِ عَنْ الْمُسْلِمِ وَاجِبٌ وَلَا يَجُوزُ أَخْذُ الْمَالِ لِيَفْعَلَ الْوَاجِبَ، اهـ مَا فِي الْفَتْحِ مُلَخَّصًا. وَفِي الْقُنْيَةِ الرِّشْوَةُ يَجِبُ رَدُّهَا وَلَا تُمْلَكُ وَفِيهَا دَفَعَ لِلْقَاضِي أَوْ لِغَيْرِهِ سُحْتًا لِإِصْلَاحِ الْمُهِمِّ فَأَصْلَحَ ثُمَّ نَدِمَ يَرُدُّ مَا دُفِعَ إلَيْهِ اهـ،

al-Fatāwā al-Hindiyya, 3:330:

الْهَدِيَّةُ مَالٌ يُعْطِيهِ وَلَا يَكُونُ مَعَهُ شَرْطٌ وَالرِّشْوَةُ مَالٌ يُعْطِيهِ بِشَرْطِ أَنْ يُعِينَهُ كَذَا فِي خِزَانَةِ الْمُفْتِينَ

Mullā Khusru, *Durar al-Ḥukkām*, 1:38:

(الْمَادَّةُ 22) :مَا أُبِيحَ لِلضَّرُورَةِ يَتَقَدَّرُ بِقَدْرِهَا. أَيْ أَنَّ الشَّيْءَ الَّذِي يَجُوزُ بِنَاءً عَلَى الضَّرُورَةِ يَجُوزُ إجْرَاؤُهُ بِالْقَدْرِ الْكَافِي لِإِزَالَةِ تِلْكَ الضَّرُورَةِ فَقَطْ، وَلَا يَجُوزُ اسْتِبَاحَتُهُ أَكْثَرَ مِمَّا تَزُولُ بِهِ الضَّرُورَةُ.

package) where there are no separate cost or charges for the coverage, then this would not be considered an independent insurance contract arrangement but an additional gift or gesture from the seller to the buyer.

- If an employer deducts from an employee's monthly salary a certain amount in return for which the employer will then pay the cost of the employee's medical treatment, then this is permitted as this is not an independent insurance contract but a condition stipulated in the employment contract; namely that the employer will cover medical costs through a monthly deduction. All conditions in Shariah contracts in origin are valid unless a clear text establishes the contrary and here there are no clear texts to prohibit such a condition.[129]

- In general, if a Muslim has entered an insurance contract already then any claims he makes cannot exceed the premiums he has paid, e.g. A has a health insurance policy of £100 premium a month. A has had the policy for 24 months (24 x £100 = £2400). If he makes a claim on this policy, he is only permitted to claim for what he has paid (£2400) as anything in surplus of this is considered *ribā*.

---

[129] Sh. `Aṭā' b. Khalīl, "Regarding Health Insurance…" available at http://www.hizb-ut-tahrir.info/arabic/index.php/HTAmeer/QAsingle/3403/:

بالنسبة للتأمين الصحي:

إذا كان ملحقا بعقد العمل أي كشرط من شروطه وليس عقداً قائماً بذاته فإنه يجوز، وإن كان عقداً بذاته فلا يجوز .وتفصيل ذلك، إذا اتفق صاحب العمل مع العامل على أن يتعهد صاحب العمل بمعالجة العامل وحده أو مع أفراد عائلته مقابل اقتطاع جزء من راتب العامل فهذا جائز، لأن العقد الأصلي هو عقد الإجارة وهذا معلوم، والتزام صاحب العمل معالجة العامل أو أفراد عائلته شرط ملحق بعقد العمل، والشروط في العقود لا تمنع إلا إذا ورد نص بمنعها كأن تحل حراماً أو تحرم حلالاً، وليست بحاجة لنص يجيزها حتى تجوز بل تحتاج إلى عدم وجود نص يمنعها، أي هي ليست كالأفعال الأصل فيها التقيد فتحتاج نصاً بجواز فعلها، بل إن شروط العقود تجوز إلا إذا ورد نص بمنعها فعن كَثِيرِ بْنِ عَبْدِ اللَّهِ بْنِ عَمْرِو بْنِ عَوْفٍ الْمُزَنِيِّ عَنْ أَبِيهِ عَنْ جَدِّهِ أَنَّ رَسُولَ اللَّهِ صَلَّى اللَّهُ عَلَيْهِ وَسَلَّمَ «وَالْمُسْلِمُونَ عَلَى شُرُوطِهِمْ إِلَّا شَرْطًا حَرَّمَ حَلَالًا أَوْ أَحَلَّ حَرَامًا» رواه الترمذي

- Accepting another person's insurance compensation (pay out) for an accident is permissible, e.g. A's car was crashed by B's reckless driving. B arranges for his insurance company to compensate for the cost of A's car. It is permissible for A to accept this compensation.

Extended Warranties

———— ♦ ————

In this section

- What warranties/extended warranties involve.
- Conventional warranty contracts.
- The Islamic viewpoint regarding warranties and extended warranties.
- Additional rulings

———— ♦ ————

Extended Warranties:

> Definition: Extended warranty insurance is taken out by consumers as protection against the failure of – or damage to – particular items, after the manufacturer's usual guarantee has expired. It is usually bought at the same time as the item in question. It may be a renewable annual contract or a policy for a fixed length of time.[130]

The underlying procedure of an extended warranty contract is as follows: A customer, A (buyer) purchases an electrical or mechanical item from a Retail store (seller), B. B offers A maintenance coverage for a possible failure of this item for a small cost or monthly fee. This fee acts as an *indemnity* (i.e. a security) against such realities as:

- General wear and tear of the item.
- Damages (including accidental).
- Failure.
- Breakage.

---

[130] Taken from, s.v. "Extended Warranties" at http://www.financial-ombudsman.org.uk/publications/technical_notes/extended-warranties.html.

- Defects in materials and workmanship.
- Replacement.
- Any other.

The Retail store may agree to exclusively offer the customer its extended warranty plan for a specified period or it may reserve the right to provide plans to more than one customer. Under the terminology of *ijāra* (hiring and leasing):

[1] The Retail store/seller/B is an **employee** (*ajīr*) of A/buyer who is the **employer** (*musta'jir*),

[2] The **subject matter** of the contract (*ma`qūd `alayh*) is the **usufruct/benefit** (*manfa`a*) the Retail store provides in its repair services (i.e. its repair work) and

[3] The **work** (*`amal*) is defined by the type of extended warranty plan taken out by the customer.

The type of employee most Retail stores are in relation to their customers/employers is a **non-exclusive contractor** (*ajīr mushtarak*) because these Retail stores also offer their services to other customers and not just one.[131]

- In *Durr al-Mukhtār* of Imām al-Ḥaṣkafī it has:

(الأجراء على ضربين : مشترك وخاص، فالأول من يعمل لا لواحد) كالخياط ونحوه (أو يعمل له عملا غير مؤقت) كأن استأجره للخياطة في بيته غير مقيدة بمدة كان أجيرا مشتركا وإن لم يعمل لغيره (أو موقتا بلا تخصيص) كأن استأجره ليرعى غنمه شهرا بدرهم كان مشتركا، إلا أن يقول: ولا ترعى غنم غيري وسيتضح.

"(The employee is of two types: *mushtarak* and *khāṣṣ*. The first type is a person who does not work for one person

[131] See *Islamic Economics and Finance: A Glossary*, ed. M. A. Khan, p.6 for the meaning of these terms.

only) like a weaver and the like (**or undertakes work for someone without a specified period of time [...] or the time is specified but not detailed)**..."[132]

(والثاني) وهو الأجير (الخاص) ويسمى أجير وحد (وهو من يعمل لواحد عملا مؤقتا بالتخصيص ويستحق الأجر بتسليم نفسه في المدة وإن لم يعمل كمن استؤجر شهرا للخدمة أو) شهرا (لرعي الغنم) المسمى بأجر مسمى بخلاف ما لو آجر المدة بأن استأجره للرعي شهرا حيث يكون مشتركا إلا إذا شرط أن لا يخدم غيره ولا يرعى لغيره فيكون خاصا وتحقيقه في الدرر وليس للخاص أن يعمل لغيره، ولو عمل نقص من أجرته بقدر ما عمل فتاوى النوازل

"(**The second type** [of employee]) **is the** ***khāṣṣ***) who is also called *ajīr wāḥid* (**and he is someone who works for one person only with a detailed specified time and is entitled to pay upon offering himself for work for a period of time)**..."[133]

- In the *Radd al-Muḥtār* of Ibn `Ābidīn it explains:

(قوله من يعمل لا لواحد) قال الزيلعي : معناه من لا يجب عليه أن يختص بواحد عمل لغيره أو لم يعمل، ولا يشترط أن يكون عاملا لغير واحد، بل إذا عمل لواحد أيضا فهو مشترك إذا كان بحيث لا يمتنع ولا يتعذر عليه أن يعمل لغيره (قوله ونحوه) أتى به وإن أغنت عنه الكاف لئلا يتوهم أنها استقصائية فافهم... قال الزيلعي : وحكمهما أي المشترك والخاص أن المشترك له أن يتقبل العمل من أشخاص لأن المعقود عليه في حقه هو العمل أو أثره فكان له أن يتقبل من العامة لأن منافعه لم تصر مستحقة لواحد ، فمن هذا الوجه سمي مشتركا والخاص لا يمكنه أن يعمل لغيره لأن منافعه في المدة صارت مستحقة للمستأجر والأجر مقابل بالمنافع ولهذا يبقى الأجر مستحقا وإن نقض العمل ا هـ

"(**His statement: a person who does not work for only one employer**). al-Zayla`ī said: this means that it is not mandatory on him to restrict himself or his work to one employer or another and neither is it a condition for him to work for more than one employer. So, even if he were to work for only a person, he would still be a *mushtarak* since

---

[132] al-Ḥaṣkafī, *Durr al-Mukhtār*, 6:64.
[133] Ibn `Ābidīn, *Radd al-Muḥtār*, 6:69-71.

there are no impediments or reasons for him to work for someone else [...] as for the *khāṣṣ*, it is not permitted for him to work for another employer because the services he offers in benefits is a for a fixed period of time entitled to the employer and his wage is commensurate with his services that is why he still gets paid even if he did not do the work properly…"

(قوله لواحد) أي لمعين واحدا أو أكثر . قال القهستاني : لو استأجر رجلان أو ثلاثة رجلا لرعي غنم لهما أو لهم خاصة كان أجيرا خاصا كما في المحيط وغيره ا هـ فخرج من له أن يعمل لغير من استأجره أولا . (قوله عملا مؤقتا) خرج من يعمل لواحد من غير توقيت كالخياط إذا عمل لواحد ولم يذكر مدة ح . (قوله بالتخصيص) خرج نحو الراعي إذا عمل لواحد عملا مؤقتا من غير أن يشرط عليه عدم العمل لغيره .

قال ط : وفيه أنه إذا استؤجر شهرا لرعي الغنم كان خاصا وإن لم يذكر التخصيص، فلعل المراد بالتخصيص أن لا يذكر عموما سواء ذكر التخصيص أو أهمله، فإن الخاص يصير مشتركا بذكر التعميم كما يأتي في عبارة الدرر (قوله وإن لم يعمل) أي إذا تمكن من العمل، فلو سلم نفسه ولم يتمكن منه لعذر كمطر ونحوه لا أجر له كما في المعراج عن الذخيرة . (قوله للخدمة) أي لخدمة المستأجر وزوجته وأولاده ووظيفته الخدمة المعتادة من السحر إلى أن تنام الناس بعد العشاء الأخيرة وأكله على المؤجر، فلو شرط على المستأجر كعلف الدابة فسد العقد كذا في كثير من الكتب، لكن قال الفقيه : في زماننا العبد يأكل من مال المستأجر حموي عن الظهيرية والخانية، وتقدم ما فيه ط : أي أول الباب السابق . (قوله أو لرعي الغنم المسمى) كذا قيده في الدرر والتبيين . وقد ذكر المصنف في الباب السابق : لو استأجر خبازا ليخبز له كذا بدرهم فسد عند الإمام لجمعه بين العمل والوقت فيخالف ما هنا، ولذا قال الشرنبلالي إذا وقع العقد على هذا الترتيب كان فاسدا كما قدمناه ، وصحته أن يلي ذكر المدة الأجر ا هـ .

قلت : وقدمنا هناك ما يقتضي وجوب حذف قوله المسمى فراجعه . (قوله وتحقيقه في الدرر) ونصه : اعلم أن الأجير للخدمة أو لرعي الغنم إنما يكون أجيرا خاصا إذا شرط عليه أن لا يخدم غيره أو لا يرعى لغيره أو ذكر المدة أولا، نحو أن يستأجر راعيا شهرا ليرعى له غنما مسماة بأجر معلوم فإنه أجير خاص بأول الكلام .

أقول : سره أنه أوقع الكلام على المدة في أوله فتكون منافعه للمستأجر في تلك المدة فيمتنع أن تكون لغيره فيها أيضا، وقوله بعد ذلك لترعى الغنم يحتمل أن يكون لإيقاع العقد على العمل فيصير أجيرا مشتركا، لأنه من يقع عقده على العمل، وأن يكون لبيان نوع العمل الواجب على الأجير الخاص في المدة ، فإن الإجارة على المدة لا تصح في الأجير الخاص ما لم يبين نوع العمل، بأن يقول : استأجرتك شهرا للخدمة أو للحصاد فلا يتغير حكم الأول بالاحتمال فيبقى أجير وحد ما لم ينص على خلافه بأن يقول : على أن ترعى غنم غيري مع غنمي وهذا ظاهر أو أخر المدة بأن استأجره ليرعى غنما مسماة له بأجر معلوم شهرا فحينئذ يكون أجيرا مشتركا بأول الكلام لإيقاع العقد على العمل في أوله، وقوله شهرا في آخر الكلام يحتمل أن يكون لإيقاع العقد على المدة فيصير أجير وحد، ويحتمل أن يكون لتقدير العمل الذي وقع العقد عليه فلا يتغير أول كلامه بالاحتمال ما لم يكن بخلافه ا هـ.

"[...] and know that the employee of a particular service or herding cattle is an *ajīr khāṣṣ* if it is made a condition that he is not permitted to offer his services to another employer or to herd another cattle of another owner with the period of time initially specified. An example is a person hired for a month to herd cattle with a designated wage. This is an *ajīr khāṣṣ* according to the first designated verbal statement..."[134]

<u>General Islamic Contract Stipulations:</u>

According to Islamic Law of contracts (refer to the chapter on Islamic contracts), a contract (`*aqd*) must have the following basic elements.

[1] Offer and acceptance (*ījāb* and *qabūl*): this is the 'pillar' (*rukn*) of the contract where a mutual exchange occurs between two parties (reciprocity) free from coercion, fraud or misrepresentation.

---

[134] Ibn `Ābidīn, *Radd al-Muḥtār*, 6:69-70.

- In *al-Badā'i` al-Ṣanā'i`* of Imām al-Kasānī it states:

وأما ركن البيع : فهو مبادلة شيء مرغوب بشيء مرغوب وذلك قد يكون بالقول وقد يكون بالفعل (أما) القول فهو المسمى بالإيجاب والقبول في عرف الفقهاء ... وأما المبادلة بالفعل فهي التعاطي ويسمى هذا البيع بيع المراوضة

"The pillar (*rukn*) of the sales contract is exchanging two desired things which can either be through verbal exchange or physical exchange. If it is a verbal exchange, then in the common terminology of the jurists it is called 'offer and acceptance' […] and if it is a physical exchange, it is called 'give and take sale' and is also known as the *murāwaḍa* sale…"[135]

[2] A subject matter of the contract: this has the following conditions:

1. Whatever is traded must be in existence at the time and not non-existent.
2. Whatever is traded must be deliverable.
3. Whatever is traded must be clearly ascertained/defined.
4. Whatever is traded must be actually owned by the seller.
5. Whatever is traded must be a permitted by the Shariah.

- In *al-Badā'i` al-Ṣanā'i`* of Imām al-Kasānī it states (condensed text):

وأما الذي يرجع إلى المعقود عليه فأنواع منها : (أن يكون موجودا فلا ينعقد بيع المعدوم) ...ومنها (أن يكون مالا لأن البيع مبادلة المال بالمال، فلا ينعقد بيع الحر لأنه ليس بمال) ... ومنها (أن يكون مملوكا لأن البيع تمليك فلا ينعقد فيما ليس بمملوك كمن باع الكلأ في أرض مملوكة، والماء الذي في نهره أو في بئره) ... ومنها (وهو شرط انعقاد البيع للبائع أن يكون مملوكا للبائع عند البيع فإن لم يكن لا ينعقد) ... ومنها (أن يكون

---

[135] al-Kasānī, *al-Badā'i` al-Ṣanā'i`*, 5:133-134.

مقدور التسليم عند العقد، فإن كان معجوز التسليم عنده لا ينعقد) ... منها (أن يكون له مجيز عند وجوده فما لا مجيز له عند وجوده لا تلحقه الإجازة) ... ومنها (قيام المالك حتى لو هلك المالك قبل إجازته لا يجوز بإجازة ورثته) . ومنها (قيام المبيع حتى لو هلك قبل إجازة المالك لا يجوز بإجازة المالك غير أنه إن هلك في يد المالك يملك بغير شيء)

"As for the subject matter of a contract, its conditions are: (1) the item must be in existence because contracting on a non-existent item is ineffective [...] (2) it has to be a valid commodity) *māl* (recognised by the Law because trade is an exchange of commodities; hence it is not permitted to sell a free person as it is not a commodity [...] (3) The item must be owned because trade involves ownership and a contract cannot be effected if there is nothing to own [...] (4) that the owner must actually own the item at the time of the sale otherwise the sale will be ineffective [...] (5) It must be deliverable at the time of the contract otherwise the contract will be ineffective [...] (6) the owner must be alive throughout the contract conclusion such that if he were to die without giving his permission, his inheritors cannot automatically present permission on his behalf [...] (7) And the object of trade must be present throughout the contract such that if it were to perish before the owner gives his permission it would not be valid..."[136]

[3] A contract that is free from *gharar* (uncertainty): i.e. excessive uncertainty relating to the subject matter of the contract, consideration (price/monies) and liabilities.

[4] A contract that is free from *ribā* (usurious elements): which is any conditional increase without corresponding consideration.

[5] A contract that is free from *qimār* (gambling elements): which is where one party's gain is conditional on the loss of another.

---

[136] al-Kasānī, *al-Badā'i' al-Ṣanā'i'*, 5:138-153.

[6] A contract must be free from *maysir*: which is a gain resulting from mere chance, speculation and conjecture and not from work or responsibility.

Basic *Ijāra* contract Stipulations:

The basic conditions related to an *ijāra* contract of employment involve the following elements:

1. **Offer and acceptance (*ījāb wa qabūl*)**: there has to be a mutual agreement between both parties as to the terms and conditions based on analogy with sale contracts because *ijāra* is an exchange of values/commodities.

2. **The duration of the employment (*mudda*)**: the period of time for which a person is available to work must be specified in order to eliminate confusion and disputes.

3. **The nature of the work (*`amal*):** the type, description and nature of the work needs to be clarified in order to ascertain what is required to remove any doubts or confusions.

4. **The wage must be deliverable**: one cannot pay someone with something known or random like birds from the sky or fish from a sea as they cannot be delivered in reality. This involves uncertainty and the Shariah seeks to avoid uncertainty.

5. **The wage of the employee**: this must be specified and determined when formulating the contract. The wage cannot be an impermissible item or impure object and it cannot be from the output of an employee.

6. **The work cannot be a religiously mandated action**: this means that one may not request a wage for an action prescribed by the law like *ṣalāt*, fasting, Zakāt, Ḥajj etc. this is in order to eliminate and remove the desire from people to do these things for the sake of Allah alone.[137]

- Imām al-Kasānī states these conditions (condensed text):

ومنها : بيان المدة في إجارة الدور والمنازل، والبيوت، والحوانيت، وفي استئجار الظئر لأن المعقود عليه لا يصير معلوم القدر بدونه، فترك بيانه يفضي إلى المنازعة، وسواء قصرت المدة أو طالت من يوم أو شهر أو سنة أو أكثر من ذلك بعد أن كانت معلومة، وهو أظهر أقوال الشافعي... ومنها : بيان العمل في استئجار الصناع والعمال لأن جهالة العمل في الاستئجار على الأعمال جهالة مفضية إلى المنازعة فيفسد العقد حتى لو استأجر عاملا ولم يسم له العمل من القصارة والخياطة والرعي ونحو ذلك لم يجز العقد، وكذا بيان المعمول فيه في الأجير المشترك، إما بالإشارة والتعيين، أو ببيان الجنس والنوع والقدر والصفة في ثوب القصارة والخياطة وبيان الجنس والقدر في إجارة الراعي من الخيل أو الإبل أو البقر أو الغنم وعددها لأن العمل يختلف باختلاف المعمول، وعلى هذا يخرج ما إذا استأجر حفارا ليحفر له بئرا أنه لا بد من بيان مكان الحفر وعمق البئر وعرضها لأن عمل الحفر يختلف باختلاف عمق المحفور وعرضه ومكان الحفر من الصلابة والرخاوة فيحتاج إلى البيان ليصير المعقود عليه معلوما، وهل يشترط فيه بيان المدة؟ أما في استئجار الراعي المشترك فيشترط لأن قدر المعقود عليه لا يصير معلوما بدونه . وأما في استئجار القصار المشترك والخياط المشترك فلا يشترط حتى لو دفع إلى خياط أو قصار أثوابا معلومة ليخيطها أو ليقصرها جاز من غير بيان المدة لأن المعقود عليه يصير معلوما بدونه . وأما في الأجير الخاص فلا يشترط بيان جنس المعمول فيه ونوعه وقدره وصفته، وإنما يشترط بيان المدة فقط ... ومنها أن يكون مقدور الاستيفاء حقيقة وشرعا لأن العقد لا يقع وسيلة إلى المعقود بدونه، فلا يجوز استئجار الآبق لأنه لا يقدر على استيفاء منفعته حقيقة لكونه معجوز التسليم حقيقة ولهذا لم يجز بيعه، ولا تجوز إجارة المغصوب من غير الغاصب، كما لا يجوز بيعه من غيره لما قلنا ... ومنها أن لا يكون العمل المستأجر له فرضا ولا واجبا على الأجير قبل

---

[137] Although scholars do differ over this issue.

الإجارة فإن كان فرضا أو واجبا عليه قبل الإجارة لم تصح الإجارة لأن من أتى بعمل يستحق عليه لا يستحق الأجرة كمن قضى دينا عليه ولهذا قلنا : إن الثواب على العبادات والقرب والطاعات أفضال من الله سبحانه غيرمستحق عليه لأن وجوبها على العبد بحق العبودية لمولاه لأن خدمة المولى على العبد مستحقة ولحق الشكر للنعم السابقة ... ومنها : أن لا يكون بالمستأجر عيب في وقت العقد أو وقت القبض يخل بالانتفاع به فإن كان لم يلزم العقد حتى قالوا في العبد المستأجر للخدمة إذا ظهر أنه سارق له أن يفسخ الإجارة لأن السلامة مشروطة دلالة فتكون كالمشروط نصا كما في بيع العين

"And one of the conditions [of the *ijāra* contract] is to clarify the time period in hiring a houses or places or residences or animals or in hiring a wet-nurse because the determined period of time cannot be known otherwise and omitting the time period will cause disputes [...] and another condition is it has to be deliverable in reality and according to the Law because the contract cannot be concluded without it thus it would not be permitted to hire or employ a runaway slave because it is not possible to benefit from it as it cannot be delivered to the involved party therefore it is not permitted to sell him [...] and another condition is to clarify the nature of the work when hiring a manufacturer or worker because uncertainty and ignorance) *jahāla* (regarding the nature of the work will lead to disputes which will cause the contract to be voidable) *yufsidu*... (because the subject matter of the contract must be known [...] and another condition is that the work one is being hired for cannot be religiously mandated work designated prior to the *ijāra* contract being drawn up because anyone who has to perform an action cannot request a wage for it ... this is why we say that the reward for doing religious worship, actions that bring one closer to Allah and general acts of obedience are all actions a worshipper has to do for Allah out of servitude to his Lord that involves gratitude for prior bounties [...] and another condition is that the hired person not possess any defects at the time of concluding the contract…"[138]

[138] al-Kasānī, *al-Badā'i` al-Ṣanā'i`*, 4:181-182. Cf. also al-Nabhānī, *The Economic System in Islam*, pp.79-104.

Islamic Viewpoint:

In relation to extended warranty plans, there are several elements that make the contract problematic from a Shariah perspective. They include:

[1] ***Gharar***: this is because the liability of the employer/customer is known but not the liability of the extended warranty service provider. The extended warranty fee – whether one payment upfront or spread over a monthly installment – is in reality a payment(s) given for a contingent future event, i.e. a possible adverse effect on the item purchased. This means that it is not certain whether the services of the extended warranty company will be required. It also means that the extent and nature of the work required and provided by the company will also be unknown. This is not acceptable in Shariah *ijāra* contracts.

In an *ijāra* employment contract, the one whose services are employed out must know the type and amount of work involved, i.e. the subject matter of the *ijāra* contract – which is the work – has to be defined. This remains unclear in an extended warranty plan because the work to be carried out is incidental repair, i.e. work contingent upon a future possibility (something that may or may not happen) and so the contracted repair technician does not know what type of work h/she will be contracted to do at any one time until notified.

In an *ijāra* employment contract, the one whose services are employed is remunerated (paid) upon completion of the specified work. However, this is not the case in an extended warranty plan where a one off payment or regular monthly payments is given in return for a set service. There is no payment made to the technician at the time of the malfunction, damage or failure of the item.

[2] ***Qimār***: If the extended warranty covers only replacements/repairs of parts then this would constitute a contingent sale, i.e. the customer will be paying a one off fee or installment fees (the price) for delivery of certain parts (subject matter of the contract) that may or may not be delivered. The uncertainty of the parts being delivered causes the contract to contain elements of *gharar*. Moreover, because one party (the customer) could suffer a loss (no repair of parts) for another party's (the retail store/seller) gain (a monetary fee) without the gain or loss specified, this constitutes *qimār* (a form of uncertainty/gambling) in trade and not acceptable according to the Shariah.

In summary, in an extended warranty contract, the Retail store selling an item is in effect offering a service to compensate the buyer/customer for a contingent loss. Thus, the buyer/customer is willing to accept a small loss (extended warranty payment) to hedge against a larger loss (damage, malfunction or breakage of the item). This makes the contract one of a conventional insurance and extremely problematic according to Shariah standards.[139]

Additional Rulings:

- A free extended warranty provided by the seller as part of the package of the product is permissible to accept.

- It would not be permitted to renew a warranty or extended warranty contract if it expires.

- Extended warranties cannot be classified as a "necessity" (*ḍarūra*) because the permissible option of paying for a technician through a call-out to fix some electrical item is available even if that option is more expensive.

---

[139] Mufti Butt, "Guarantees and Extended Warranties" available at http://alqalam.org.uk/wp-content/uploads/Guarantees-and-Extended-Warranties.pdf.

- Extended warranties cannot be justified based on the argument that this is what retailers customarily do or what financial industries consider standard practice because the Shariah is the criterion to accept or reject customary practice or any form of standards.

Forex Trading (*online/electronic*)

Forex Trading

1. Forex Trading (online/electronic).

Chapter 7

♦

Forex Trading (online)

In this section

- What Forex trading involves.
- Islamic conventional currency trading.
- The Islamic viewpoint regarding online Forex trading.
- Additional rulings

Forex Trading:

Essentially Forex online trading (FX) is when a person buys and simultaneously sells a pair of currencies based on a *speculation* through a *broker*. In other words, he trades in £, $ and ¥, etc. anticipating the rise in value of the currency (*appreciation*) to gain a profit. The two currencies involved in the currency trade are called a *currency pair*. The most common pairs that make up most of the international volume of currency (appr. 80%) trading are:

1. €/$ EUR/USD = EUR.
2. £/$ GBP/USD = POUND.
3. $/$ USD/CAD = CANADIAN DOLLAR.
4. $/¥ USD/YEN = YEN.
5. $/CHF = SWISS FRANC
6. $/$ AUD/USD = AUSSIE.

The first currency (on the left) is called the *base* currency whereas the second currency (on the right) is called the *counter* or *quote* currency. Each currency pair is expressed in units of the counter currency needed to get one unit of the base currency. If the price or quote of the €/$-EUR/USD pair is 1.345, it means that 1.345 US dollars are needed to get one EUR. When a currency is bought, it is referred to as *going long* and when selling, it is referred to as *going short*. The price at which you buy is called *ask* and the price at which you sell is called a *bid*. The difference between the ask price and the bid price is known as the *forex spread*. If A buys €, then at the same, time he sells $USD because they are a pair. Again, if A buys £, then at the same time he sells $USD because they are a pair and the same holds for all other currency pairs.

Forex trading is typically carried out through a broker or market maker who takes the proposed trade and puts it on the open market for a mandatory and specified fee. **Example**: A is a forex trader. A chooses a currency pair that he expects (or speculates) to positively change in value and places a trade accordingly. Thus, A purchases, say, €1,000 in January of 2009 and it cost him around $1,200 USD. He then tracks the value over the year such that by December 2009 the €'s value vs. the $'s value increased to $1,300 USD, i.e. for every €1,000 he could now get $1,300 USD. If A chose to end his trade at that point, he would have made a $100 gain.

Another pivotal feature of Forex trading is *leverage*. This simply means a person is given more currency by a forex broker to trade with than what he actually has in his account. In this way, a forex trader could stand to gain more because he has more currency and a broker potentially gains more in his fee % because the trading values are higher. For instance, if a forex brokerage offers 50:1 leverage, that means for every £1 that is in a person's account, he can trade £50 on the forex market.

Islamic Conventional Currency Trading (*al-ṣarf*):

It is permissible to trade one currency with another[140] provided there is cognisance of the following scenarios:

1. *When there is no possession*: If, party A and party B are trading currencies but neither actually gains possession of the respective currency from the other, then this is not permissible because no exchange of counter-values has taken place.

2. *When both parties gain possession*: If, party A and party B are trading currencies and both actually gain possession of the respective currencies, then this is permissible and the currencies may be subsequently sold at any rate.

3. *When one party gains possession*: If, party A and party B are trading currencies and there is <u>no agreed date of a deferred payment</u>, then this is permissible and the currencies may be sold/exchanged at any rate.[141] If there <u>is an agreement for a date for a deferred payment</u>, then currencies can only be sold for the current market rate otherwise it would be tantamount to an interest-bearing transaction.

"Therefore, one currency may be traded for another at any rate, as long as one party takes possession in the same gathering. However, in the case where the contract stipulates deferred payment on one side, the currencies may only be traded at their current market rate."[142] If currency exchanges

---

[140] See al-Nabhānī, *The Economic System in Islam*, pp.249-252.

[141] al-Bukhārī, *al-Muḥīṭ al-Burhānī*, 9:296:

ذكر محمد رحمه الله تعالى هذه المسألة في صرف الأصل ولم يشترط التقابض فهذا دليل على أن التقابض ليس بشرط...لأن التقابض مع العينة إنما يشترط في الصرف وهذا ليس بصرف

[142] See R. al-Būṭī, *al-Buyū` al-Shā'i`a*, pp.308-369 and Mufti A. Mirza, "Could you please clarify the rules of purchasing gold, silver and

are in this manner, then it is permissible according to Shariah.[143]

currencies…" response given at http://askimam.org/public/question_detail/21027#_ftn7

[143] al-Bukhārī, *al-Muḥīṭ al-Burhānī*, 9:296:

ثم إذا باع فلساً بعينه بفلسين بأعيانهما حتى جاز العقد عند أبي حنيفة، هل يشترط التقابض في المجلس؟ ذكر محمد رحمه الله هذه المسألة في صرف «الأصل»ولم يشترط التقابض فهذا دليل على أن التقابض ليس بشرط، وذكر في «الجامع الصغير»: ما يدل على أنه شرط. فإنه قال: إذا باع فلساً بفلسين يجوز يداً بيد إذا كان بعينه من مشايخنا من لم يصحح ما ذكر في «الجامع الصغير»: لأن التقابض مع العينية إنما يشترط في الصرف وهذا ليس بصرف، ومن مشايخنا من صحح ما ذكر في «الجامع الصغير»لأن الفلوس لها حكم العروض من وجه وحكم الأثمان من وجه، فمن حيث إن لها حكم العروض جوزنا بيع واحد باثنين إذا كان عينين كما لو باع سيفاً بسيفين، ومن حيث إن لها حكم الدرهم شرطه التقابض في المجلس صح العينية عملاً بالدليلين بقدر الإمكان. وذكر القدوري في «شرحه»: إذا باع الفلس بالفلس وقبض أحدهما ما اشترى ولم يقبض الآخر حتى تفرقا، أو تقابضا ثم استحق ما في يد أحدهما بعد الافتراق، فالعقد صحيح على حاله

al-Kasānī, *al-Badā'i` al-Ṣanā'i`*, 4:487-488:

كذا إذا تبايعا فلسا بعينه بفلس بعينه فالفلسان لا يتعينان وإن عينا إلا أن القبض في المجلس شرط حتى يبطل بترك التقابض في المجلس لكونه افتراقا عن دين بدين ولو قبض أحد البدلين في المجلس فافترقا قبل قبض الآخر ذكر الكرخي أنه لا يبطل العقد لأن اشتراط القبض من الجانبين من خصائص الصرف وهذا ليس بصرف فيكتفي فيه بالقبض من أحد الجانبين لأن به يخرج عن كونه افتراقا عن دين بدين وذكر في بعض شروح مختصر الطحاوي رحمه الله أنه يبطل لا لكونه صرفا بل لتمكن ربا النساء فيه لوجود أحد وصفي علة ربا الفضل وهو الجنس وهو الصحيح

al-Fatāwā al-Hindiyya, 3:224:

لو باع الفلوس بالفلوس ثم افترقا قبل التقابض بطل البيع ولو قبض أحدهما ولم يقبض الآخر أو تقابضا ثم استحق ما في يدي أحدهما بعد الافتراق فالعقد صحيح على حاله كذا في الحاوي

Islamic Viewpoint:

Forex trading online as a Shariah compliant mode of trading is complicated due to a number of ambiguous elements in the trading modality:

[1] Currency possession: it is not altogether clear whether a forex trader actually has possession (*qabḍ*) of real currency if he is trading with forex leverage because what occurs is that a trader is given an inflated currency value beyond what he actually possesses in his account. Hence, he is trading with items he neither owns nor actually possesses (or perhaps does not even exist) which is not permitted in Shariah.[144]

[2] Trading with debt: it is not clear whether the leverage through a forex broker is a form of debt incurred by the forex trader which is then exchanged on the forex market. If several traders are in the market trading with debts then in effect, there will be exchanges of debts on both sides (by buyers and sellers) and it is well known that the Prophet forbade a sale of a debt for a debt (*bay` al-dayn bi'l-dayn*).[145]

[3] Trading with interest-bearing loans: Usually, when trading on the forex market with leverage, this appears to be a loan given by a broker to the trader. Such loans have been gained on interest (*ribā*) taken out on behalf of a trader. In Shariah, however, to authorise or be part of a usurious transaction is not permitted.

---

[144] Muḥammad al-Shaybānī, *Kitāb al-Aṣl*, 5:31:

لَا يجوز أَن يَبِيع مَا لم يقبض وَقد جَاءَ قي الْأَثر عَن رَسُول الله صلى الله عَلَيْهِ وَسلم أَنه نهى عَن بيع الرجل مَا لم يقبض

[145] `Abd al-Razzāq, *al-Muṣannaf*, 9:80:

أخبرنا عبد الرزاق قال أخبرنا الأسلمي قال حدثنا عبد الله بن دينار عن بن عمر قال نهى رسول الله صلى الله عليه و سلم عن بيع الكالىء وهو بيع الدين بالدين

[4] Combining two contracts in one: one other reason that renders Forex trading problematic is the conflation of two contracts in one. Thus, when trading with leverage, a sale and purchase contract (of currencies) is made conditional upon credit (loan). In other words, for a person to buy and sell currency, they need to get a credit (a loan) so a sale/purchase contract is combined with a loan contract. This would not be permitted.

Other objections include:

- Excessive speculating is against Islamic practice.
- Excessive uncertainty in trading which is against Islamic Law.
- Making currency into a commodity is contrary to Islamic financial ethics.
- Participating in a usurious contract is not permitted.

Although at this moment in time, some contemporary scholars appear to be undecided on the categorical prohibition of Forex trading, the ambiguous elements are sufficient for many scholars to warrant abstention from entering into it until a thorough and scholarly assessment is made or clearer Shariah-compliant manoeuvres are in place.

Derivative Financial Contracts

Derivative Financial Contracts

1. Forward Contracts
2. Futures Transactions
3. Options Trading
4. Conclusion

Chapter 8

♦

Forward Contracts, Futures Transactions and Options Transactions (الاختيارات)

In this section

- What Forward contracts involve.
- The Islamic viewpoint regarding Forward transactions.

What Forward Contracts Involve:

Definition: A forward contract is an agreement between two parties to exchange at some fixed future date a given quantity of a commodity for a price defined today. The fixed price today is known as the *forward price*. Islamic Forward Contracts are made with the express intention of delivering the currency on the specified future date. In common practice it is called a 'sale'.

In a conventional forward contract where both payment and delivery is made at a future date is deemed un-Islamic, as the transaction is agreed and binding whereas both payment and delivery remains uncertain. The conventional "deferred contract" therefore carries the potential losses to one party. Generally, the forward purchase is not considered to be permissible as it contravenes the general rule 'do not sell what you do not own', an established principle of Islamic jurisprudence. Therefore the normal contract for shorting shares is not permissible under *Shariah* rules.[146]

In other words, the underlying contractual scheme is as follows:

A agrees with B to sell some asset/commodity *x* for an agreed price of £100 at a future date (say in three months time/March 2009). When March arrives, the delivery of *x* will be made in exchange for the price to complete the transaction.

Often, such contracts are made to hedge against risk – especially in the fluctuation of prices. If for example, a cocoa farmer (producer/seller) expects to harvest 100 tons of cocoa in six months time by June 2009 and a confectioner (consumer/buyer) estimates he will need cocoa by that time, in such a scenario, both the farmer and the confectioner can agree on a price now to conclude in June. This is carried out to reduce price risk. The farmer does not want the price to fall over time and the confectioner does not want the price to rise so both face a risk in opposite directions. By locking in a price deal now, both can take advantage of any price fluctuations as well as plan their business activities and make assurances to suppliers and customers.

Islamic Viewpoint:

[1] No exchange of counter-values: Forward contracts – like all contracts of this type – are contrary to Shariah laws pertaining to a valid contract because there has to be an immediate and absolute exchange of counter-values, i.e. the

---

[146] Jamaldeen, "Futures, Forwards and Islamic Law" available at http://ziaahmedkhan.hubpages.com/hub/Futures-Forwards-and-Islamic-Law. See also idem, *Islamic Finance*, p.183; Al-Bashir, *Risk Management in Islamic Finance*, pp.15-35 and Kamali, *Islamic Commercial Law*, pp.1-13.

buyer must receive delivery of the goods and the seller must receive the price.[147] This does not occur in a forward sale. Mufti Taqi Usmani comments on this point:

> The futures transactions in vogue in stock and commodities markets today is not permissible for two reasons. Firstly, it is a well recognized principle of the Shariah that sale or purchase cannot be affected for a future date. Therefore, all Forward and Futures transactions are invalid in Shariah [...][148]

---

[147] al-Mawṣilī, *al-Ikhtiyār li-Ta`līl al-Mukhtār*, 2:269:

قال: (ولو باع عينا على أن يسلمها إلى رأس الشهر فهو فاسد) لأن تأجيل الأعيان باطل إذ لا فائدة فيه، لأن التأجيل شرع في الأثمان ترفها عليه ليتمكن من تحصيله وأنه معدوم في الأعيان فكان شرطا فاسدا

[148] Mufti Taqi Usmani, "Futures, Options and Swaps" in *International Journal of Islamic Financial Services*, vol.1, no. 1, p.36 available at http://www.meezanbank.com. See also the discussions on Futures transactions below for further details.

Futures Transactions

In this section

- What Futures transactions involve.
- The Islamic viewpoint regarding Futures transactions.

What Futures Involves:

> Definition: In finance, a futures contract (more colloquially, *futures*) is a standardized contract between two parties to buy or sell a specified asset of standardized quantity and quality for a price agreed upon today (the *futures price* or *strike price*) with delivery and payment occurring at a specified future date, the *delivery date*. The contracts are negotiated at a futures exchange, which acts as an intermediary between the two parties. The party agreeing to buy the underlying asset in the future, the "buyer" of the contract, is said to be "long", and the party agreeing to sell the asset in the future, the "seller" of the contract, is said to be "short". The terminology reflects the expectations of the parties—the buyer hopes or expects that the asset price is going to increase, while the seller hopes or expects that it will decrease in near future.[149]

Futures transactions developed over time out of the shortcomings of Forward sales and is often seen as a standardised sub-set of it.[150]

---

[149] From "Futures Contract" available at http://en.wikipedia.org/wiki/Futures_contract

[150] Kamali, *Islamic Commercial Law*, pp.15-48.

Example: A agrees to purchase a fungible commodity or asset (e.g. wheat, grain, oil, etc.) from B for £1000 today January 2009 in a Commodities Exchange Market (CEM) whether directly or through a broker. Both A and B agree delivery of the asset/commodity as well as payment for March 2009. Both parties conduct the transaction based on an expectation of appreciation and depreciation in value of the asset/commodity. A (buyer) expects an increase in the asset/commodity price beyond £1000 whereas B (Seller) expects it to decrease. If for example between January and March 2009, the price of the fungible commodity/asset appreciates (goes up) to £1,200 and B secures a deal to sell for £1,100, he has made £100 profit. So the difference between the buy and sell figure was £100. If, however, the price depreciates (goes down) to £900 and the expiration date of the contract arrives, B will suffer a loss of £100.

The Futures trading risk is amplified by something called *leverage*. What this refers to is:

> …having control over large cash amounts of commodities with comparatively small levels of capital. In other words, with a relatively small amount of cash, you can enter into a futures contract that is worth much more than you initially have to pay (deposit into your margin account). It is said that in the futures market, more than any other form of investment, price changes are highly leveraged, meaning a small change in a futures price can translate into a huge gain or loss.

Leverage is a 'double-edged-sword' where the possibility of huge gains comes with the risks of huge losses:

> Futures positions are highly leveraged because the initial margins that are set by the exchanges are relatively small compared to the cash value of the

contracts in question (which is part of the reason why the futures market is useful but also very risky). The smaller the margin in relation to the cash value of the futures contract, the higher the leverage. So for an initial margin of $5,000, you may be able to enter into a long position in a futures contract for 30,000 pounds of coffee valued at $50,000, which would be considered highly leveraged investments…

Highly leveraged investments can produce two results: great profits or greater losses. As a result, of leverage, if the price of the futures contract moves up even slightly, the profit gain will be large in comparison to the initial margin. However, if the price just inches downwards, that same high leverage will yield huge losses in comparison to the initial margin deposit. For example, say that in anticipation of a rise in stock prices across the board, you buy a futures contract with a margin deposit of $10,000, for an index currently standing at 1300. The value of the contract is worth $250 times the index (e.g. $250 x 1300 = $325,000), meaning that for every point gain or loss, $250 will be gained or lost. If after a couple of months, the index realized a gain of 5%, this would mean the index gained 65 points to stand at 1365. In terms of money, this would mean that you as an investor earned a profit of $16,250 (65 points x $250); a profit of 162%!

On the other hand, if the index declined 5%, it would result in a monetary loss of $16,250 - a huge amount compared to the initial margin deposit made to obtain the contract. This means you still have to pay $6,250 out of your pocket to cover your losses. The fact that a small change of 5% to the index could result in such a large profit or loss to the investor (sometimes even more than the initial investment made) is the risky arithmetic of leverage. Consequently, while the value of a commodity or a financial instrument may not exhibit very much price volatility, the same

> percentage gains and losses are much more dramatic in futures contracts due to low margins and high leverage.[151]

Although the above is a very simplified account of Futures trading, nevertheless the essence is the same. There are intricate rules that govern the process and procedure of Futures trading and can develop into complicated transaction sequences with innumerable simultaneous transactions over a period of time, concluded electronically. Nevertheless, the core idea underpinning Futures trading is again heavy speculation, leverage and selling without actual possession or delivery of the subject-matter of the sale.

Islamic Viewpoint:

Futures transactions characterised in this way are seen as extremely problematic according to Shariah due to the following:

[1] Lack of possession: in most futures trading behaviour, traders are involved in 'paper trading', i.e. they are not concerned with actually transferring ownership of an underlying commodity/asset, i.e. to gain possession (*qabḍ*) of it. Hence, parties are trading with items they neither own nor possesses (whether actually or constructively) which is not permitted in Shariah.[152]

[2] Contravenes key principles of sale: one of the recognised principles of Shariah contracts is that a sale must

---

[151] "Futures Fundamentals: Characteristics" available at http://www.investopedia.com/university/futures/futures4.asp

[152] Muḥammad al-Shaybānī, *Kitāb al-Aṣl*, 5:31:

لَا يجوز أَن يَبِيع مَا لم يقبض وَقد جَاءَ قي الْأَثر عَن رَسُول الله صلى الله عَلَيْهِ وَسلم أَنه نهى عَن بيع الرجل مَا لم يقبض

be instant and absolute. Complete sales cannot be attributed to a future date and they cannot be made contingent on a future event. **Example 1**: A states to B <u>today</u> that he will sell something to B <u>next month</u>. This is a sale based on a future date, which is not permissible. **Example 2**: A states to B that he will sell some item if such and such event occurs in the future, e.g. A says: 'I will sell this item to you if this football team wins the Primer League'. This is a sale based on a *future contingent*, which is not permissible either.[153]

[3] Exchanging debts: Because futures transactions involve deferment to a future specified date, the sale and the price offered for the sale become unfulfilled promises (because they have not been realised in an immediate exchange). In other words, the seller still owes the buyer a commodity/asset and the buyer still owes the seller a price; thus this state of owing is a debt (*dayn*) on both sides and the Shariah prohibits an exchange of debt contract (*bay` al-dayn bi 'l-dayn*).[154]

---

[153] Ibn `Ābidīn, *Radd al-Muḥtār*, 4:531:

لأن تأجيل المبيع المعين لا يجوز ويفسده بحر

[154] al-Ḥākim *al-Mustadrak*, 2:57 and `Abd al-Razzāq, *al-Muṣannaf*, 9:80:

أخبرنا عبد الرزاق قال أخبرنا الأسلمي قال حدثنا عبد الله بن دينار عن بن عمر قال : نهى رسول الله صلى الله عليه و سلم عن بيع الكالىء وهو بيع الدين بالدين

See for example Mufti Taqi Usmani's comments in "Futures, Options and Swaps" in *International Journal of Islamic Financial Services*, vol.1, no. 1, pp.36-39 available at http://www.meezanbank.com; A. Salehabadi and M. Aram, "Islamic Justification of Derivative Instruments" in *International Journal of Islamic Financial Services*, vol.4, no.3 available at http://www.iefpedia.com; "Futures: Halal or Haram?" available at http://www.ilmfruits.com/2009/futures-halal-or-haram/ as well as Mufti Ibn Adam's "Foreign Exchange Trading" available at http://www.daruliftaa.com. Cf. Kamali, *Islamic Commercial Law*, pp.125-130.

For a detailed discussion on Futures and the scholarly dispute surrounding it, refer to M. A. Ehsan, *Islamic Perspectives on Financial*

[4] No delivery: In most of the Futures transactions, delivery of a commodity/asset or their possession is not the primary objective. In most cases, these transactions are closed with settlement of difference in prices; more precisely, it is used for excessive speculation purposes and speculation is contrary to Shariah principles of commerce and trade.

<u>Other objections include</u>:

- Misallocation of resources.
- Excessive speculating is against Islamic practice.
- Excessive uncertainty in trading which is against Islamic Law.
- Monopoly and exploitation of smaller traders by larger companies.
- Leverage as a problematic element in trading because low margin trading generates speculation and exponential loss.
- Hedging as a tool to offset risk or loss is problematic according to Shariah.
- Very few contracts are actually held to delivery because of offsetting prior to contract expiration.

Derivatives (PhD thesis submitted to Durham University, 2012), pp.104-122; Kamali, *Islamic Commercial Law*, pp.66-158; idem, "Commodity Futures: An Islamic Legal Analysis," *Thunderbird International Business Review*, vol. 49 , No. 3 (April), pp.309-339; M. Al-Bashir, *Risk Management in Islamic Finance*, pp.14-34 and 121-193 and J. Iqbal, *Islamic Financial Management*, pp.5-12.

Options Transactions

(الاختيارات)

In this section

- What Options transactions involve.
- The Islamic viewpoint regarding Options transactions.

What Options Involve:

> Definition: An option is a contract that gives the buyer the right, but not the obligation, to buy or sell an underlying asset at a specific price on or before a certain date. An option, just like a stock or bond, is a security. It is also a binding contract with strictly defined terms and properties...[155]

Example: A (buyer) wants to purchase a house from B (seller). The house costs £250,000 today in January 2009. A does not have that money now but will have it within three month (March 2009). A negotiates with B the purchase of the house in March for £250,000 but that option to purchase it in March comes at a fee/cost of £2000. If March arrives and A changes his mind and retracts from purchasing the house, A will lose £2000 and will not be legally obligated to complete the sale.

[155] "Options Basics: What are Options?" available at http://www.investopedia.com/university/options/option.asp.

Mufti Ibn Adam outlines the underlying schema of the transaction and summarises the ruling of the prohibition of Options transactions as follows:

> An option is a contractual agreement that gives the holder the right to buy (*call option*) or sell (*put option*) a fixed quantity of a security or commodity at a fixed price, within a specified period of time.
>
> For example: A promises B that he will purchase a specific commodity for £100 at any time between the 1st of January and the 1st of March. B will have the right to sell that particular commodity to A for £100 within that period, but he will not be obligated, although if he does desire to do so, A will be obligated to purchase it. This option (of sale) which B has is known as the "put option". If however, A promised B that he will sell him a specific commodity for £100 during a specific time, if B desired to purchase it, then this will be known as the "call option". Here the holder of the option (B) has a right to buy the commodity whenever he desires during that fixed period, although he will not be obligated to do so. The one giving the option (or promising to buy or sell) will charge a fee for his promise and service.
>
> Options contracts are not only restricted to commodities, rather one can also purchase options on future contracts, interest rates and currencies in the same way. The price one pays for the option is called the "premium" and the price at which it is agreed that one may buy or sell the commodity, etc… is called the "exercise price".
>
> The objective behind these option contracts is to guarantee oneself from the fall in the prices of commodities and currencies. For example: A purchased one British pound for two dollars. Now, he fears that if he keeps this pound in his possession, the value of the pound may fall in the future, thus he will suffer loss. But, at the same time, if he was to sell his pound at present, he may

well deprive himself of potential profit, for the price of the pound may rise in the future. Therefore, he enters into a options agreement where he purchases an option to sell his pound for two dollars for a specific period, thus if the price of the pound rises he will sell it in the market, and if it falls, he has the option to sell it for two dollars to the person from whom he purchased the option. Moreover, these options have become an article of trade themselves, where individuals further sell these options to others in the options market.

From a Shariah perspective, options contracts are also unlawful (*haram*) and not permissible. The reason being is that a promise to sell or purchase is in itself permissible and is morally binding upon the promisor, but this promise cannot be a subject matter of a sale or purchase. In other words, it will not be permissible to charge a fee for making such a promise.

Similarly, it will not be permissible to further sell these options, for they are not something that can be traded in. An intangible object cannot be a subject of sale according to the *Fuqaha'* except with certain conditions, which are not met here.

Furthermore, there is an element of interest (*riba*) in these contracts. The extra fee charged by the one who makes the promise is in addition to the price of the commodity. This is more relevant where currency is being traded in. For the above reasons, Shaykh Mufti Taqi Usmani (may Allah preserve him) issued the following Fatwa in his *Contemporary Fatwa*:

"Since the prevalent options transactions in the options market are based on charging fees on these promises, they are not valid according to Shariah. This ruling applies to all kinds of options, no matter whether they are call options or put options. Similarly, it makes no difference if the subject matter of the option sale is a commodity, gold or

> silver, or a currency; and as the contract is invalid *ab-initio*, the same cannot be transferred." (See: *Contemporary Fatawa*, p. 152).[156]

The Fiqh Academy Resolution No. 63 (1/7) regarding Options is as follows:[157]

ثانياً: الاختيارات:

أ. صورة عقود الاختيارات:

إن المقصود بعقود الاختيارات الاعتياض عن الالتزام ببيع شيء محدد موصوف أو شرائه بسعر محدد خلال فترة زمنية معينة أوفي وقت معين إما مباشرة أو من خلال هيئة ضامنة لحقوق الطرفين.

ب.حكمها الشرعي:

إن عقود الاختيارات –كما تجري اليوم في الأسواق المالية العالمية – هي عقود مستحدثة لا تنضوي تحت أي عقد من العقود الشرعية المسماة.

وبما أن المعقود عليه ليس مالاً ولا منفعة ولا حقاً مالياً يجوز الاعتياض عنه فإنه عقد غير جائز شرعاً.

وبما أن هذه العقود لا تجوز ابتداءً فلا يجوز تداولها.

The AAOIFI Standard on the Sale of Commodities in Organised Markets has the following on Options trading:[158]

---

[156] See "Foreign Exchange Trading" available at http://spa.qibla.com with slight changes.

[157] Journal no. 6, 2:1273, no.7, 1:73 and no.9, 2:5 (= p.131 [English]).

[158] AAOIFI, *Standard*, p.356.

5/2/1:

A contract by means of which a right is bestowed – but not an obligation – for the purchase or sale of an identified item (like shares, commodities, currencies, indexes or debts) at a determined price and for a deferment period. There is no obligation in this contract except on the person selling this right.

5/2/2:

Option contracts indicated above are not permitted neither with respect to their formation nor trading.

12.

The basis for the impermissibility of options is that the subject-matter of the contract in them is not wealth that can be deemed compensation according to the Sharia.[159]

There are Shariah substitutes proposed by the AAOIFI based on *`ārbūn*, *khiyār al-sharṭ* and *al-wa`d al-mulzim*:[160]

5/2/3:

Shariah Substitutes for Options

5/2/3/1:

The conclusion of a contract pertaining to ascertained assets is permitted according to Sharia, along with the payment of part of the price as earnest money (*`ārbūn*) with the stipulation that the buyer has the right to revoke the contract within a specified period in lieu of the entitlement of the seller to the amount of earnest money in

---

[159] Ibid., 'Appendix B', p.362.
[160] Ibid., p.357.

case the buyer exercises his right of revocation. It is not permitted to trade the right established with respect to the earnest money.

5/2/3/2:

The conclusion of a contract for commodities in themselves along with the stipulation of an option for establishing the right of revocation for one of the parties, or for both, during a known period. This option is not eligible for trading.

5/2/3/3:

The issuance of a binding promise by the owner of assets to sell them, or a binding promise by one desiring to buy them, without specifying a counter-value for the promise. The promise is not eligible for trading.

Islamic Viewpoint:

Options transactions characterised in this way are thus highly problematic according to Shariah due to the following reasons:[161]

[1] Making a promise a subject of sale: it is not permitted in Shariah to make something intangible like a right a subject-matter of a sale/contract. Charging a fee therefore for a securing a promise (something intangible) is not permitted as a subject-matter of a sale or purchase.[162]

[2] Trading in Options: similar to point [1] above, selling on Options contract to another party is not permissible as this

---

[161] Cf. Ehsan, *Islamic Perspectives on Financial Derivatives*, pp.122-130 and Al-Bashir, *Risk Management in Islamic Finance*, pp.195-221.
[162] Kamali, *Islamic Commercial Law*, p.139.

is trading in an intangible commodity and this is not permitted in Shariah.[163]

[3] Intrusion of interest: charging a fee for securing an Option is tantamount to *ribā* because it is an unwarranted addition (surplus) gained on the price of the asset/commodity under consideration.[164]

Conclusion:

Therefore, Muslim scholars are extremely wary of derivatives as a mode finance or investment for the following reasons:

- It is based on excessive speculation which is contrary to Shariah principles of trading.
- It is based on *ribā*.[165]
- It is based on *gharar*.
- It is based on selling items without actual or constructive possession (*qabḍ ḥaqīqī*/*qabḍ ḥukmī*) between traders. Hence, many derivatives contracts involve 'paper sales' without actual delivery of commodities.
- It is based on making money a commodity.[166]
- It is based on leverage which is an instrument tantamount to gambling.

---

[163] Ibid., pp.99-109.

[164] Ibid., pp.196-197.

[165] Ehsan, *Islamic Perspective on Financial Derivatives*, p.128.

[166] Ibid., p.128. I have omitted the swaps as a mode of Islamic derivatives instrument because it is not a contract individuals predominantly enter into but large companies. For Shariah-compliant swaps proposals, see S. Yankson, "Derivatives in Islamic Finance – A Case for Profit Rate Swaps" in *Journal of Islamic Economics, Banking and Finance*, vol.7, no. 1 (Jan-Mar), 2011, pp.39-56 and M. Ayub, "Use of Wa`d and Tawarruq for Swaps in the Framework of Islamic Finance", paper at the 8th International Conference on Islamic Economics and Finance available at http://conference.qfis.edu.qa/app/media/317.

- It is based on margin trading which is not Shariah compliant. The Fiqh Council passed the following Resolution regarding this:

After listening to the research that has been submitted and the detailed discussion on this topic, the opinion of the council is that this transaction involves the following:

1. Dealing in buying and selling for the purpose of profit, and this dealing is usually done in major currencies or financial certificates (shares and bonds) or some types of products, and it may include trade in options, futures and the indexes of major markets.

2. Loans, which refers to the money given by the agent to the customer directly if the agent is a bank, or via a third party if the agent is not a bank.

3. *Riba*, which occurs in this transaction in the form of fees for delaying the deal. This is interest that is charged to the purchaser if he does not make a decision on the same day, and which may be a percentage of the loan or a set amount.

4. Commission, which is the money that the agent gets as a result of the investor's (customer's) dealing through him, and it is an agreed-upon percentage of the value of the sale or purchase.

5. The pledge, which is a commitment signed by the customer agreeing to leave the contract with the agent as a pledge for a loan, giving him the right to sell these contracts and take back the loan if the customer's losses reach a specific percentage of the margin, unless the customer increases the pledge in order to compensate for a drop in the price of the product.

The Committee believes that this transaction is not permissible according to Shari`ah for the following reasons:

Firstly: It involves obvious *riba,* which is represented by the addition to the amount of the loan which is called "paying fees for delaying the deal". This is a kind of *haram riba.* Allah says (interpretation of the meaning):

{***O you who believe! Fear Allah and give up what remains of riba if you are believers / And if you do not do it, then take a notice of war from Allah and His Messenger but if you repent, you shall have your capital sums. Deal not unjustly, and you shall not be dealt with unjustly (by receiving less than your capital sums***)."[167]

Secondly: The agent stipulates that the customer must deal through him, which leads to combining both giving a loan for something in return and paying commission, which is akin to combining giving a loan and selling at the same time, which is forbidden in Shari`ah because the Messenger said: **"It is not permissible to give a loan and sell at the same time…"** The *hadith* was narrated by Abu Dawud (3/384) and al-Tirmidhi (3/526), who said it is a *hasan sahih hadith.* In this case he has benefited from his loan, and the *fuqaha'* are unanimously agreed that every loan that brings a benefit is *haram riba.*

Thirdly: Dealings that are done in this manner in the global markets usually involve many contracts that are *haram* according to Shari`ah, such as:

1. Dealing in bonds, which comes under the heading of *riba* which is *haram.* This was stated in a resolution of the Islamic Fiqh Council in Jeddah, no. 60, in its sixth session.

---

[167] See Q. 2:278-279.

2. Dealing indiscriminately in company shares. The fourth statement of the Islamic Fiqh Council of the Muslim World League in its fourteenth session in 1415 AH stated that it is *haram* to deal in the shares of companies whose main purposes are *haram*, or some of their dealings involve *riba*.

3. Selling currencies is usually done without the hand to hand exchange which makes them permissible according to Shari`ah.

4. Dealing in options and futures. A resolution of the Islamic Fiqh Council in Jeddah no. (63), in its sixth session, stated that options are not permissible according to Shari`ah, because the object of dealing in these contracts is not money or services or a financial obligation which it is permissible to exchange. The same applies to futures and trading in indexes.

5. In some cases the agent is selling something that he does not possess, and selling what one does not possess is forbidden in Shari`ah.

Fourthly: This transaction involves economic harm to the parties involved, especially the customer (investor), and to the economy of the society in general, because it is based on borrowing to excess and taking risks. Such matters usually involve cheating, misleading people, rumours, hoarding, artificial inflation of prices and rapid and strong fluctuation of prices, with the aim of getting rich quickly and acquiring the savings of others in unlawful ways. Hence it comes under the heading of consuming people's wealth unlawfully, in addition to diverting wealth in society from real, fruitful economic activity to this type of risk that has no economic advantage, and it may lead to severe economic turmoil that will cause great loss and harm in society.

The Council advises financial institutions to follow the ways of finance that are prescribed in Shari`ah and that do not involve *riba* and the like, and do not have harmful economic effects on their customers or on the economy in general, like *shar`i* partnerships and the like. And Allah is the Source of strength.[168]

The Arabic text is as follows:

وبعد الاستماع إلى البحوث التي قدمت، والمناقشات المستفيضة حول الموضوع، رأى المجلس أن هذه المعاملة تشتمل على الآتي:

1. المتاجرة (البيع والشراء بهدف الربح)، وهذه المتاجرة تتم غالباً في العملات الرئيسية، أو الأوراق المالية (الأسهم والسندات)، أو بعض أنواع السلع، وقد تشمل عقود الخيارات ، وعقود المستقبليات، والتجارة في مؤشرات الأسواق الرئيسة .
2. القرض ، وهو المبلغ الذي يقدمه الوسيط للعميل مباشرة إن كان الوسيط مصرفاً ، أو بواسطة طرف آخر إن كان الوسيط ليس مصرفاً .
3. الربا، ويقع في هذه المعاملة من طريق (رسوم التبييت)، وهي الفائدة المشروطة على المستثمر إذا لم يتصرف في الصفقة في اليوم نفسه، والتي قد تكون نسبة مئوية من القرض، أو مبلغاً مقطوعاً.
4. السمسرة، وهي المبلغ الذي يحصل عليه الوسيط نتيجة متاجرة المستثمر (العميل) عن طريقه ، وهي نسبة متفق عليها من قيمة البيع أو الشراء .
5. الرهن، وهو الالتزام الذي وقعه العميل بإبقاء عقود المتاجرة لدى الوسيط رهناً بمبلغ القرض، وإعطائه الحق في بيع هذه العقود واستيفاء القرض إذا وصلت خسارة العميل إلى نسبة محددة من مبلغ الهامش، ما لم يقم العميل بزيادة الرهن بما يقابل انخفاض سعر السلعة.

---

[168] 2:229. Taken from islamqa.com with minor alterations.

ويرى المجلس أن هذه المعاملة لا تجوز شرعاً للأسباب الآتية:

أولاً : ما اشتملت عليه من الربا الصريح ، المتمثل في الزيادة على مبلغ القرض، المسماة (رسوم التبييت)، فهي من الربا المحرم، قال تعالى:

(يَا أَيُّهَا الَّذِينَ آمَنُوا اتَّقُوا اللَّهَ وَذَرُوا مَا بَقِيَ مِنَ الرِّبا إِنْ كُنْتُمْ مُؤْمِنِينَ * فَإِنْ لَمْ تَفْعَلُوا فَأْذَنُوا بِحَرْبٍ مِنَ اللَّهِ وَرَسُولِهِ وَإِنْ تُبْتُمْ فَلَكُمْ رُؤُوسُ أَمْوَالِكُمْ لا تَظْلِمُونَ وَلا تُظْلَمُونَ) البقرة/**278**، **279** .

ثانيا: أن اشتراط الوسيط على العميل أن تكون تجارته عن طريقه، يؤدي إلى الجمع بين سلف ومعاوضة (السمسرة)، وهو في معنى الجمع بين سلف وبيع، المنهي عنه شرعاً في قول الرسول صلى الله عليه وسلم: (لا يحل سلف وبيع ...) الحديث رواه أبو داود (**384/3**) والترمذي (**526/3**) وقال: حديث حسن صحيح . وهو بهذا يكون قد انتفع من قرضه ، وقد اتفق الفقهاء على أن كل قرض جر نفعاً فهو من الربا المحرم .

ثالثاً : أن المتاجرة التي تتم في هذه المعاملة في الأسواق العالمية غالباً ما تشتمل على كثير من العقود المحرمة شرعاً، ومن ذلك :

1. المتاجرة في السندات، وهي من الربا المحرم، وقد نص على هذا قرار مجمع الفقه الإسلامي بجدة رقم (**60**) في دورته السادسة .
2. المتاجرة في أسهم الشركات دون تمييز، وقد نص القرار الرابع للمجمع الفقهي الإسلامي برابطة العالم الإسلامي في دورته الرابعة عشرة سنة **1415**هـ على حرمة المتاجرة في أسهم الشركات التي غرضها الأساسي محرم، أو بعض معاملاتها ربا .
3. بيع وشراء العملات يتم غالباً دون قبض شرعي يجيز التصرف .
4. التجارة في عقود الخيار وعقود المستقبليات، وقد نص قرار مجمع الفقه الإسلامي بجدة رقم (**63**) في دورته السادسة، أن عقود الخيارات غير جائزة شرعاً، لأن المعقود عليه ليس مالاً ولا منفعة ولا حقاً مالياً يجوز الاعتياض عنه .. ومثلها عقود المستقبليات والعقد على المؤشر .
5. أن الوسيط في بعض الحالات يبيع ما لا يملك ، وبيع ما لا يملك ممنوع شرعاً .

رابعاً : لما تشتمل عليه هذه المعاملة من أضرار اقتصادية على الأطراف المتعاملة، وخصوصاً العميل (المستثمر)، وعلى اقتصاد المجتمع بصفة عامة . لأنها تقوم على التوسع في الديون، وعلى المجازفة، وما تشتمل عليه غالباً من خداع وتضليل وشائعات، واحتكار ونجش وتقلبات قوية وسريعة للأسعار، بهدف الثراء السريع والحصول على مدخرات الآخرين بطرق غير مشروعة، مما يجعلها من قبيل أكل المال بالباطل، إضافة إلى تحويل الأموال في المجتمع من الأنشطة الاقتصادية الحقيقية المثمرة إلى هذه المجازفات غير المثمرة اقتصاديا، وقد تؤدي إلى هزات اقتصادية عنيفة تلحق بالمجتمع خسائر وأضرار فادحة .

ويوصي المجمع المؤسسات المالية باتباع طرق التمويل المشروعة التي لا تتضمن الربا أو شبهته ، ولا تحدث آثاراً اقتصادية ضارة بعملائها أو بالاقتصاد العام كالمشاركات الشرعية ونحوها ، والله ولي التوفيق .

Thus:

> Essentially, futures and other derivatives are matters of disparity among scholars. The large majority of scholars, among them members of OIC Fiqh academy and Fiqh academy in Mecca, hold derivatives to be impermissible. Reasons for such verdict may be summarized in three groups: firstly, derivatives involve oppressive and prohibited elements like *gharar*, speculations and gambling, future contracts are large paper transaction not genuine purchases or sales, sale what the seller does not own, sale of debt for debt, selling prior possession (without any physical transfer or delivery), subject matter is unacceptable, etc.
>
> Furthermore, conservative scholars claimed that derivatives cannot be driven out as any traditional contract in Shariah. Lastly, derivatives cause great harm to people, causing price distortion (price is not determined by market forces) and financial crises. For these reasons they are forbidden. If

majority of scholars clearly agreed that derivatives should be prohibited, further question could be raised: does Islamic finance need derivatives contracts and their risky, uncertain and speculative way of performance?

Looking from the input and output point of view, this uncertain and speculative behavior of futures contracts had led to discovery of various hedging devices. If Shariah has clearly defined the basic principles of Islamic contracts, which prohibits uncertainty and speculation, does Islamic finance really needs hedging devices? The reality is that risk management is entrenched in the Islamic law of contract and financial transactions such that if they are really applied as endowed, there is essentially no actual need to elaborate the concern of risk in the manner it is practiced in the conventional model. Thus, the principal question to address is whether all that needs to be pursued in mode of *Maqasid Shariah* are essentially realized.

Additionally, some conservative scholars have voiced their serious consternation at the conduct(s) and manners Islamic finance has been performed of late. They are particularly questioning a "blind" following of conventional financial engineering. Recent mortgage market collapse is, to a great extent, based on financial derivatives, distressed the fundamentals of conventional finance. In other hand, Islamic finance was extremely resilient, particularly owing to Shariah and its principles (*Maqasid Shariah*). If Islamic finance confidently follows their conventional peers in development and applications of future contracts and hedging instruments, shall the next financial crisis come from Islamic world?

In view of this, and in the light of the Shariah principle of permissibility that makes all commercial transactions permissible in the absence of a clear prohibition, the rulings of not only the

Mecca based Fiqh Academy but also of many Muslim scholars who have proscribed futures contracts disallowed is a most discouraging form of imitation. This firm opinion is founded on the analysis that futures contracts do not fulfil the requirements of the conventional Islamic law of contract. From above discussion, it could be concluded that contemporary trading in derivatives is impermissible as it includes prohibited categories of sale of debts, *riba* and it is a field in which artificial finance industry builds it basis. However, taking into consideration the need of Islamic finance for efficient hedging methods, there is believe that use of some derivatives for mere hedging purposes may be accepted provided some important adjustments.[169]

---

[169] Taken from M. Vejzagic's article "Future Contracts: Islamic Contract Law Perspective", pp.29-31 available at http://www.academia.edu with minor typographical corrections.

Some Personal Finance *Schemes*

Some Personal Finance Schemes:

1. Murābaḥa Transactions (Cost-Plus).

2. Tawarruq Transactions (reverse Murābaḥa).

3. Shariah-Compliant Home Plans

Chapter 9

Murābaḥa (المرابحة), *Tawarruq* (التورق / Monetisation) and Islamic Home Purchase Schemes

In this section

- What *Murābaḥa* involves.
- Basic rules of *Murābaḥa*.
- The Islamic viewpoint regarding *Murābaḥa*.

What *Murābaḥa* involves:

From the Arabic root *r* / *b* / *ḥ* / meaning 'gain' or 'profit'.[170] Jamaldeen explains *Murābaḥa* as follows:

> In murabaha agreements, a commodity is sold for cost plus profit, and both the buyer and seller know the cost and the profit involved. The customer can make a lump payment when the commodity is delivered but usually sets up a deferred payment installment schedule.
>
> For example, say a manufacturer wants to buy $100,000 worth of wood but doesn't have enough funds. The manufacturer approaches the bank and signs an agreement to purchase the wood from the bank at cost ($100,000) plus profit (maybe 20 percent of the contract amount, or $20,000).

[170] Lane, *Lexicon*, Book.1, pp.1008-1009.

> The manufacturer is liable to pay the bank $120,000 after the bank delivers the goods. Both parties know the profit and the cost of the product at the onset; there's no financial uncertainty in the transaction.[171]

The basic outline of the transaction is: A buys *x* from B where B sells *x* to A with a mark-up and disclosure of the mark-up %, e.g. B sells a car to A for £10,000 where the original price (cost-price) was £7,000 with a profit figure of £3,000 totalling £10,000.

Often, *Murābaḥa* is used as both a personal finance method as well as a mode of finance for banks. Below is the basic algorithm of this transaction between a buyer, seller and an Islamic bank:

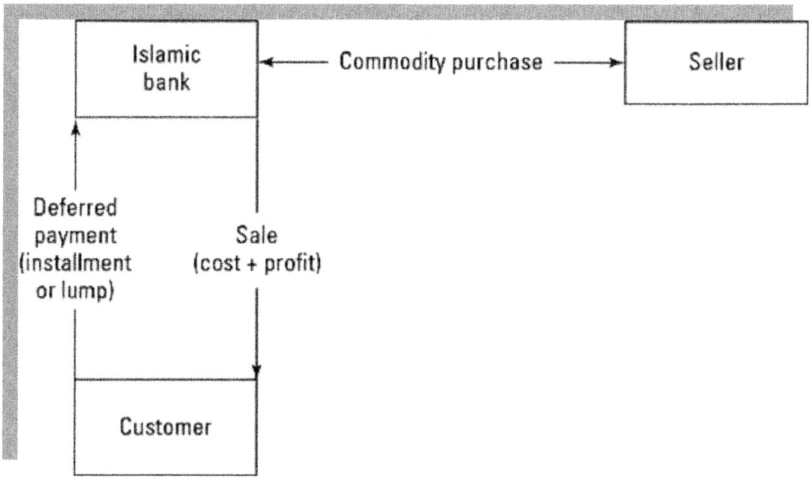

fig.2. a schema of a *Murābaḥa* transaction
(source: Jamaldeen, *Islamic Finance*)

---

[171] Jamaldeen, *Islamic Finance*, p.154. See also Mufti Taqi Usmani, *An Introduction to Islamic Finance*, pp.65-109; Kettell, *Islamic Finance*, pp.24-36; Schoon, *Islamic Banking and Finance,* pp.69-77; pp.141-156 M. Çizakça, *Islamic Capitalism and Finance*, pp.141-156 and Abdulkader, *Structuring Islamic Finance*, pp.60-75.

Some argue that *Murābaḥa* is simply a synthesised loan (i.e. a loan divided into pieces) whereas this is a misconception. In fact, *Murābaḥa* is a sale contract; thus, there is trading of an actual commodity or asset and so it is not a loan contract where money is exchanged for more money with no real economic activity. The financier in the *Murābaḥa* sale (e.g. a Bank) takes risk and responsibility so is not profiting from a mere risk-free venture.

Basic rules of *Murābaḥa*:

According to Mufti Taqi Usmani, the requirements of the *Murābaḥa* include minimally the following:[172]

1. *Murabahah* is not a loan given on interest. It is the sale of a commodity for a deferred price, which includes an agreed profit added to the cost.

2. Being a sale, and not a loan, the *murabahah* should fulfil all the conditions necessary for a valid sale, especially those enumerated earlier in this chapter.

3. *Murabahah* cannot be used as a mode of financing except where the client needs funds to actually purchase some commodities. For example, if he wants funds to purchase cotton as a raw material for his ginning factory, the Bank can sell him the cotton on the basis of *murabahah*. But, where the funds are required for some other purposes, like paying the price of commodities already purchased by him, or the bills of electricity or other utilities or for paying the salaries of his staff, *murabahah* cannot be effected, because *murabahah* requires a real sale of some commodities, and not merely advancing a loan.

4. The financier must have owned the commodity before he sells it to his client.

---

[172] Taken from *An Introduction to Islamic Finance*, pp.73-75 with minor typological amendments. Cf. also al-Kasānī, *al-Badā'i` al-Ṣanā'i`*, 5:220-222.

5. The commodity must come into the possession of the financier, whether physical or constructive, in the sense that the commodity must be in his risk, though for a short period.

6. The best way for *murabahah*, according to Shariah, is that the financier himself purchases the commodity and keeps it in his own possession, or purchases the commodity through a third person appointed by him as agent, before he sells it to the customer. However, in exceptional cases, where direct purchase from the supplier is not practicable for some reason, it is also allowed that he makes the customer himself his agent to buy the commodity on his behalf. In this case, the client first purchases the commodity on behalf of his financier and takes its possession as such. Thereafter, he purchases the commodity from the financier for a deferred price His possession over the commodity in the first instance is in the capacity of an agent of his financier. In this capacity, he is only a trustee, while the ownership vests in the financier and the risk of the commodity is also borne by him as a logical consequence of the ownership. But, when the client purchases the commodity from his financier, the ownership, as well as the risk, is transferred to the client.

7. As mentioned earlier, the sale cannot take place unless the commodity comes into the possession of the seller, but the seller can promise to sell even when the commodity is not in his possession. The same rule is applicable to *murabahah*.

8. It is also a necessary condition for the validity of *murabahah* that the commodity is purchased from a third party. The purchase of the commodity from the client himself on 'buy back' agreement is not allowed in Shariah. Thus, *murabahah* based on 'buy back' agreement is nothing more than an interest based transaction.

Other rules include:

9. **If the client defaults on the payment, the financier isn't allowed to charge extra fees as late payment or penalty charges.** Sharia scholars allow charging additional fees in cases of loss or damage due to a client's default, and they allow certain penalties to ensure that a buyer is not negligent. But such fees and penalties cannot be treated as income for the bank; they must be given to charity.

10. **The contract should be used only for purchases.** It's not intended to be used for financing a working capital requirement.[173]

The Islamic viewpoint regarding *Murābaḥa*:

In general, the scholars permit *Murābaḥa* transactions although they have cautioned that it is not exactly a mode of finance even if it is utilised as one by Islamic banks.

[173] Taken verbatim from Jamaldeen, *Islamic Finance*, p.154.

Tawarruq (التورق / Monetisation)

♦

In this section

- What *Tawarruq* involves.
- Organised *Tawarruq*.
- The Islamic viewpoint regarding *Tawarruq*.

What *Tawarruq* involves:

The word comes from the Arabic root *w / r / q /* meaning 'silver coins'[174] and so the transaction is about generating equity.

> Definition: *Tawarruq* is a financial instrument in which a buyer purchases a commodity from a seller on a deferred payment basis, and the buyer sells the same commodity to a third party on a *spot payment* basis (meaning that payment is made on the spot). The buyer basically borrows the cash needed to make the initial purchase. Later, when he secures the cash from the second transaction, the buyer pays the original seller the installment or lump sum payment he owes (which is cost plus markup, or *murabaha*). Because the buyer has a contract for a *murabaha* transaction, and later the same transaction is reversed, this scenario is called a *reverse murabaha.* Both transactions involved must be sharia-compliant.[175]

The basic steps of the classical *Tawarruq* contract is as follows:

---

[174] Lane, *Lexicon*, Suppl.1, p.3051-3052.
[175] Taken from Jamaldeen, *Islamic Finance*, p.156.

First: A (buyer/*mustawriq*) enters into a commodity cost-plus sale (*murabaha*) with an Islamic Bank, B (seller) for the amount of £10,000.

Second: A sells what he purchased from B to a third party buyer, C for immediate cash in a spot sale for £8,000.

Third: A now takes this ready cash and uses it to pay back the arrangement he made with B.

What seems to be taking place then in this type of *Tawarruq* transaction is that goods obtained on credit are sold for its spot value in order not to gain possession of the goods, but to gain liquidity. This linear form of *Tawarruq* (known as *al-tawarruq al-fardī* or 'real *tawarruq*') is considered permissible by all legal Schools although some prominent classical jurists have expressed their dislike in how it is really a manoeuvre to circumvent *ribā*.[176]

Below is a diagram outlining an Islamic Bank's *modus operandi* of real *Tawarruq*:

---

[176] See for example Mufti Taqi Usmani's "Verdicts on at-Tawarruq and its Banking Applications", pp.1-28 available at http://uaelaws.files.wordpress.com/2012/08/verdicts-on-tawarruq.pdf and A. Ajija et al, "Tawarruq: Issues and Challenges", pp.10-17 for a brief juristic discussion on the contract in medieval *fiqh* books. See also s.v. "Tawarruq" available at http://www.qfinance.com; S. Khan, "Organised Tawarruq in Practice: A Shariah Non-Compliant and Unjustified Transaction" available at http://www.newhorizon-islamicbanking.com; A. al-Hadad, "Tawarruq, Its Essence and Types: Mainstream Tawarruq and Organised Tawarruq", pp.1-20 available at http://www.kantakji.com; "Tawarruq: A Brief Overview available at http://www.azamlaw.com; al-Munajjid, "Tawarruq via the Bank and Differences in Fatwas Concerning it from Fiqh Councils and Banks' Scholars" available at http://islamqa.info/en/98124 and "Tawarruq" available at http://wiki.islamicfinance.de/index.php/Tawarruq.

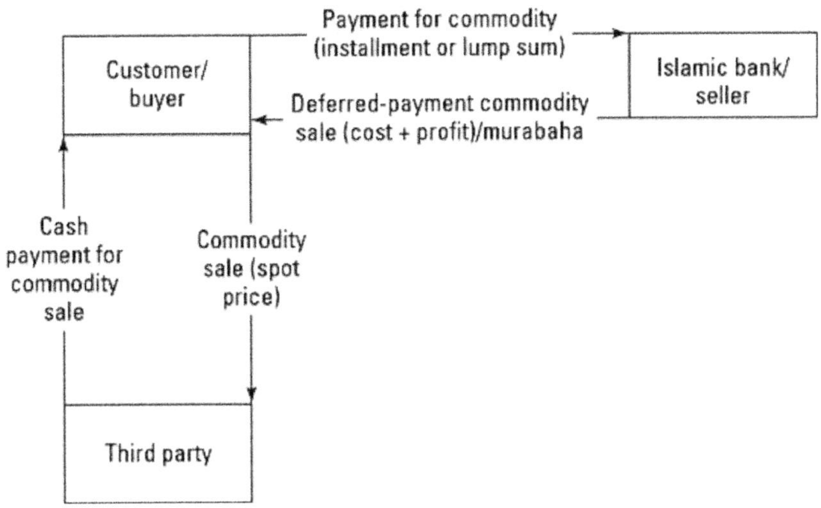

fig.3. a schema of a *Tawarruq* transaction
(source: Jamaldeen, *Islamic Finance*)

Organised *Tawarruq*:

Another major type of *Tawarruq* contract used by many Islamic banks as a mode of finance is Organised *Tawarruq*. This involves the following type of financing scheme:

A (a customer) approaches B (an Islamic Bank) for money. B suggests to A that he purchase *x* for, say, £1100. A purchases *x* for £1100 from B on a deferred agreement of 12 months instalment payments. A then appoints B as his client to sell *x* on the market for a spot cash price of £1000 to a third party C. B then transfers the cash of £1000 to A who then pays back B in instalments.[177]

Shalhoob summarises the problem with organised *Tawarruq* as follows:

[177] M. Y. Saleem, *Islamic Commercial Law*, pp.26-29.

Looking carefully at the contract of the organised *tawarruq*, it can be argued that there is no difference, in terms of aim and result, between it and usury in Islamic law. To clarify the point, assume that there are two clients who want to be financed for any reason; the first client applies for a loan with interest, which is a form of usury by way of deferment in Islamic law, and he borrows £10,000 for £11,000 to be paid within two years. Then the second person applies for financing by organised *tawarruq* to buy copper from the financial institution for £11,000 to be paid within two years. The client knows that the financial institution has bought the copper from the international market for £10,000, and the financial institution will sell the copper in the international market on behalf of the client for £10,000. As shown, there is no difference between the forms in term of the aim, which is to finance the client, and the result, which is to charge the client more than what he receives. In addition, financing by organised *tawarruq* may cost the clients more than taking a loan with interest, because in the latter case the financial institution lends to the client directly instead of engaging in a long procedure to buy commodities and sells them again in the same market. Thus, the loan with interest may be processed faster than the organised *tawarruq*, because the client may obtain money directly after the contract, whereas the client who asks to be financed through the organised *tawarruq* would have to wait until the commodities are sold in the market.[178]

Islamic Viewpoint:

Regarding the status of *tawarruq*, the OIC in its resolution 179 (5/19) in Sharjah, United Arab Emirates, from

[178] S. al-Shalhoob, "Organised Tawarruq in Islamic Law", pp.10-11 available at http://faculty.kfupm.edu.sa/IAS/shalhoob.

1-5 of Jumādī al-Ūlā 1430 AH, corresponding to 26–30 April 2009 stated the following:

قرار رقم **179** (**5/19**)

بشأن التورق: حقيقته وأنواعه (الفقهي المعروف والمصرفي المنظم)

الحمد لله رب العالمين والصلاة والسلام على سيدنا محمد خاتم النبيين وعلى آله وصحبه أجمعين إن مجلس مجمع الفقه الإسلامي الدولي المنبثق عن منظمة المؤتمر الإسلامي المنعقد في دورته التاسعة عشرة في إمارة الشارقة (دولة الإمارات العربية المتحدة) من **1** إلى **5** جمادى الأولى **1430**هـ، الموافق **26** – **30** نيسان (إبريل) **2009**م.

بعد اطلاعه على البحوث الواردة إلى المجمع بخصوص موضوع التورق: حقيقته، أنواعه (الفقهي المعروف والمصرفي المنظم)، وبعد استماعه إلى المناقشات التي دارت حوله، وبعد الاطلاع على قرارات المجمع الفقهي الإسلامي التابع لرابطة العالم الإسلامي بمكة المكرمة بهذا الخصوص...

قرر ما يلي :

أولاً: أنواع التورق وأحكامها :

(**1**) التورق في اصطلاح الفقهاء: هو شراء شخص (المستورق) سلعة بثمن مؤجل من أجل أن يبيعها نقداً بثمن أقل غالباً إلى غير من اشتُريت منه بقصد الحصول على النقد. وهذا التورق جائز شرعاً، شرط أن يكون مستوفياً لشروط البيع المقررة شرعاً .

(2) التورق المنظم في الاصطلاح المعاصر: هو شراء المستورق سلعة من الأسواق المحلية أو الدولية أو ما شابهها بثمن مؤجل يتولى البائع (المموّل) ترتيب بيعها، إما بنفسه أو بتوكيل غيره أو بتواطؤ المستورق مع البائع على ذلك، وذلك بثمن حال أقل غالباً .

(3) التورق العكسي: هو صورة التورق المنظم نفسها مع كون المستورق هو المؤسسة والممول هو العميل. ثانياً: لا يجوز التورقان (المنظم و العكسي) وذلك لأن فيهما تواطؤاً

بين الممول والمستورق، صراحة أو ضمناً أو عرفاً، تحايلاً لتحصيل النقد الحاضر بأكثر منه في الذمة وهو ربا.

ويوصي بما يلي :

(أ) التأكيد على المصارف والمؤسسات المالية الإسلامية باستخدام صيغ الاستثمار والتمويل المشروعة في جميع أعمالها، وتجنب الصيغ المحرمة والمشبوهة التزاماً بالضوابط الشرعية بما يحقق مقاصد الشريعة الغراء، ويجلي فضيلة الاقتصاد الإسلامي للعالم الذي يعاني من التقلبات والكوارث الاقتصادية المرة تلو الأخرى

(ب) التأكيد القرض الحسن لتجنيب المحتاجين للجوء للتورق و الإنشاء المؤسسات المالية الإسلامية صناديق للقرض الحسن...

Translation:

Having reviewed the research papers that were presented to the Council regarding the topic of *tawarruq*, its meaning and its type (classical applications and organized *tawarruq*), a resolution were passed. Furthermore, after listening to the discussions that revolved about the applications of *tawarruq*, the resolutions were presented at the International Council of Fiqh Academy, under auspices of the Muslim World League in Makkah. The following were the resolutions:

First: Types of *tawarruq* and its juristic rulings: Technically, according to the *Fiqh* jurists, *tawarruq* can be defined as: a person (*mustawriq*) who buys a merchandise at a deferred price, in order to sell it in cash at a lower price. Usually, he sells the merchandise to a third party, with the aim to obtain cash. This is the classical *tawarruq*, which is permissible, provided that it complies with the Shariah requirements on sale (*bay*`).

The contemporary definition on organized *tawarruq* is: when a person (*mustawriq*) buys a merchandise from a local or international market on deferred price basis. The financier arranges the sale agreement either himself or through his agent. Simultaneously, the *mustawriq* and the financier executes the transactions, usually at a lower spot price.

Reverse *tawarruq*: it is similar to organized *tawarruq*, but in this case, the (*mustawriq*) is the financial institution, and it acts as a client.

Second: It is not permissible to execute both *tawarruq* (organised and reversed) because simultaneous transactions occurs between the financier and the *mustawriq*, whether it is done explicitly or implicitly or based on common practice, in exchange for a financial obligation. This is considered a deception, i.e. in order to get the additional quick cash from the contract. Hence, the transaction is considered as containing the element of *ribā*.

The recommendation is as follows: To ensure that Islamic banking and financial institutions adopt investment and financing techniques that are Shariah-compliant in all its activities, they should avoid all dubious and prohibited financial techniques, in order to conform to Shariah rules and so that the techniques will ensure the actualization of the Shariah objectives (*maqāṣid al-sharī`ah*). Furthermore, it will also ensure that the progress and actualization of the socioeconomic objectives of the Muslim world. If the current situation is not rectified, the Muslim world would continue to face serious challenges and economic imbalances that will never end.

To encourage the financial institutions to provide *qarḍ ḥasan* (benevolent loans) to needy customers in order to discourage them from relying on *tawarruq* instead *of qarḍ ḥasan.* Again these institutions are encouraged to set up special *qarḍ ḥasan* Fund.[179]

In general, scholars do not see anything problematic with the classical *Tawarruq* contract outlined in the beginning of the chapter but the commercialised forms employed by Islamic banks for finance purposes are deemed highly problematic and therefore not Shariah-compliant:

- **Disguised *ribā***: *Tawarruq* and other comparable debt instruments are dressing up interest-based debt instruments and thus undermine Shariah ethical finance and its socio-economic objectives because they contain strong elements of a riskless transaction with secured returns.[180]

- **No economic activity**: merely establishing networks of *Tawarruq* trade contracts without any real or constructive possession of goods is argued as increasing equity with little or no real economic activity. This again is akin to – or encourages – *ribā*. It also means that there is no real and ultimate end user of the sold commodity. It is merely activity registered in transactions databases and financial books and nothing more.[181]

- **Identical to *bay` al-`īna***: this type of contract was already outlined in the chapter on invalid contracts. Some scholars equate the organised *Tawarruq* with *bay` al-`īna* which is not a permitted form of sale as it in essence involves exchanging money for money with an additional sum.[182]

---

[179] See Resolution no. 179 (5/19), 19th Session, pp.12-13.
[180] Khan, "Organised Tawarruq in Practice".
[181] Ibid.
[182] Ibid.

- **No possession**: In organised *Tawarruq* arrangements, it is not clear wither the client gains any real possession of the commodity before selling it for immediate cash especially if the Islamic bank is both financier and third party buyer/seller because there are in most cases no storage receipts, demarcations or evidence of actual ownership transfer. Thus, the commodity appears to be acting as a prop from hidden monetisation transactions that virtually never moves giving rise to an absence of genuine trade and contravening the condition of goods needing to be owned or possessed before they are sold.[183]

---

[183] Ibid.

Islamic Home Purchase Schemes

♦

In this section

- Conventional Home Loans.
- Basic rules of Loans in Islam.
- Diminishing *Mushāraka* Scheme (DMS), Murābaḥa Housing Scheme (MHS) and the 'Ijāra Muntahiya bi 'l-Tamlīk Programme (IMT).
- The Islamic viewpoint regarding Islamic Home Purchase Schemes.

Conventional Home Loans:

In a conventional home loan or mortgage, a person borrows money from a bank to purchase a property with an upfront deposit that constitutes a % of the overall value and agrees to repay the remaining value of the property over a number of years with interest. The borrower pledges the house to the bank that has legal claims over the property in case of defaults on payment at which point the bank can evict the tenant, foreclose, seize the property and then sell it to compensate for the outstanding mortgage amount. What this type of contract amounts to, then, is a form of debt instrument that is secured by the collateral of a specified property.

Example: A approaches a Bank, B to purchase a house for £200,000. A puts down a deposit of £40,000 (20%) and the bank offers the remaining £160,000 (80%) value of the property known as the Loan to Value (LTV). A agrees to pay back the loan to B over say 20 or 25 years with monthly payments plus an interest charge (whether fixed or variable). In this way, the principal is cleared with interest.

Conventional interest bearing loans of this type are unlawful in Islam due to the explicit interest on the loan. Ibn Qudāma writes:

وكل قرض شرط فيه أن يزيده فهو حرام بغير خلاف. قال ابن المنذر: أجمعوا على أن المُسلف إذا شرط على المستلف زيادة أو هدية، فأسلف على ذلك أن أخذ الزيادة على ذلك ربا. وقد روي عن أبي بن كعب وابن عباس وابن مسعود أنهم نهوا عن قرض جر منفعة...

"Every loan that contains a condition for a surplus is unlawful without any scholarly dispute. Ibn al-Mundhir said: They [s: the scholars] are unanimously agreed that if the lender stipulates that the borrower must pay extra or give a gift and he gives the loan on this basis, this is *ribā*. It was narrated from Ubayy b. Ka`b, Ibn `Abbās and Ibn Mas`ūd that they forbade loans that lead to any kind of benefit..."[184]

Basic Rules of Loans in Islam:

The Islamic view is that the lender cannot benefit in any way from lending; he has no privileged position by merely being a lender or financier. The general rules related to loans (*qarḍ*)[185] in the Shariah are:

1. Loans like any contracts must be concluded through valid offer and acceptance.[186]

2. Contracting parties must be legally fit and suitable to enter into a contract, e.g. in possession of their mental faculties.[187]

---

[184] Ibn Qudāma, *al-Mughnī*, 6:436.
[185] Linguistically it means 'cutting off a piece of something' or 'cutting of a portion'. Hence, a loan is like giving borrower part or portion of what one owns. See Lane, *Lexicon*, Bk.1, p.2516.
[186] al-Zuḥaylī, *Financial Transactions*, 1:374.
[187] Ibid., 1:374.

3. Loans can be of fungible and non-fungible goods (any object that incurs legal liability) as long as it is an object that is permissible in the Shariah.[188]

4. Whatever is leant, it amount (e.g. volume, weight, quantity, size, etc.) must be known in order to make repayment in equivalence possible.[189]

5. No benefit may be stipulated as a condition on the loan whether monetary as this constitutes *ribā* or qualitative as this would fall under the prohibition of conducting a loan and a sale in one contract.[190]

In order to offer home finance products that are thus *ribā*-free or avoid any unwarranted benefits to the lender (and hence an alternative to conventional mortgages), Islamic banks have a number of structured mortgage

---

[188] Ibid., 1:375.
[189] Ibid., 1:375.
[190] Ibid., 1:376-378. The Prophet said: **"A sale with a loan (*salaf*) is not permitted..."** Abū Dāwud (#3504) and Tirmidhī (#1234) in their *Sunan*:

لا يحل سلف وبيع

The commentator of Tirmidhī's *Sunan* states:

قَالَ الْقَاضِي رَحِمَهُ اللَّهُ : أَيْ : لَا يَحِلُّ بَيْعٌ مَعَ شَرْطِ سَلَفٍ، بِأَنْ يَقُولَ مَثَلًا : بِعْتُك هَذَا الثَّوْبَ بِعَشْرَةٍ عَلَى أَنْ تُقْرِضَنِي عَشْرَةً

"al-Qāḍī (may Allah have mercy on him) said: i.e., 'it is not permissible to sell with the condition of a loan, by saying for example': 'I will sell this garment to you for ten on the basis that you lend me ten'...", al-Mubārakfūrī, *Tuḥfat al-Aḥwadhī*, 4:361.

Ibn Taymiyya stated the consensus on the prohibition of a sale contract with a loan, *al-Majmū` al-Fatāwā*, 30:83:

وَقَدْ اتَّفَقَ الْفُقَهَاءُ عَلَى أَنَّهُ لَا يَجُوزُ أَنْ يَشْرِطَ مَعَ الْبَيْعِ عَقْدًا مِثْلَ هَذَا؛ فَلَا يَجُوزُ أَنْ يَبِيعَهُ عَلَى أَنْ يُقْرِضَهُ

"The jurists are unanimous on the point that it is not permissible to stipulate with the sale a contract such as this, so it is not permissible to sell to him on the basis that he gives him a loan..."

schemes that are also adopted by some retail banks as part of their personal finance services. Below will be a basic analysis of three of these common alternatives: the 'Diminishing Mushāraka Scheme' (DMS), The Murābaḥa Housing Scheme (MHS) and the Ijāra Muntahiya bi 'l-Tamlīk (IMT) programme.[191]

Diminishing *Mushāraka* Scheme (DMS/المشاركة المتناقصة):

Also known as "reduced balance partnership" or "declining balance co-ownership programme", DM schemes are explained as follows:

> Diminishing Musharakah is a form of partnership, which ends with the complete ownership of a partner who purchases the share of another partner in that project by a redeeming mechanism agreed between both of them. Diminishing Musharakah is used mostly when one party who wants to own an asset or a commercial business which does not have adequate funds to pay the full price; and takes the assistance of financing from another party. The share of the financier is divided into a number of units and it is understood that the client will purchase the units of the share of the financier one by one periodically, thus increasing his own share till all the units of the financier are purchased by the client so as to make him the sole owner of the asset. In this kind of partnership, all partners are co-owners of each and every part of the joint property or asset on a pro-rata basis and one partner cannot make a claim to a specific part of the property or asset leaving the other parts for other partners.[192]

[191] M. Maurer, *Pious Property: Islamic Mortgages in the United States*, Ch.2 and D. Loundy, "Islamic Mortgages" in K. Hunt-Ahmed, ed. *Contemporary Islamic Finance: Innovations, Applications and Best Practice*, pp.283-292.

[192] Quoted from http://www.financialislam.com/diminishing-musharakah1.html with some minor adjustments.

Another explanation is as follows:

> Diminishing Musharakah also known as **Shirkah-ul- Mutanaqisah** is a form co-ownership in which two or more partners share the ownership of business or tangible asset in identified proportion where one or more partner undertake to buy the shares of the partners gradually in instalments until the title of such business or tangible asset is completely owned by the buying partner(s).
>
> The Diminishing Musharakah is a permissible participatory Shariah compliant mode of finance which is developed near past extracted from Musharakah mode of finance. This mode of finance complies with Islamic ethics and consideration. It is also an optional (*al-khiyar*) contract which tends to reduce or remove Gharar in managing business by making one partner the sole owner of that business.
>
> In Diminishing Musharakah, the participants (financier and its clients) in either the joint ownership of the asset or joint commercial enterprise have an agreement that the financier will sell its share to the client which is divided into number of units to be sold one by one in specific interval. The process of buying the unit shares increases the share of the client until he becomes the sole owner of that property or commercial enterprise.[193]

The HM Revenue and Customs website describes the DM scheme as:

---

[193] M. Dabiri, *Diminishing Musharaka: Islamic Financial Instrument Manual*, paper submitted to the Institute of Islamic Finance Academy for Modern International Studies, Kent, 2012, p.9.

This product involves the use of two written contracts, being a lease agreement ('Ijara') and a diminishing ownership agreement ('Musharaka'), where two or more parties share ownership of an asset.

Example: A customer wishes to purchase a residential property for £200,000. He/she pays a deposit of £20,000 to the vendor of the property and then enters into a diminishing ownership agreement with the bank, under which the bank pays the outstanding £180,000, taking title to the property by way of a sub-sale between the vendor and the bank. The bank's customer now has a 10% beneficial interest (or share) in the property, with the remainder being with the bank. The bank allows the customer to defer payment of the £180,000 over a period of twenty-five years. It does not (and cannot) add any interest to the £180,000 and so under this contract the customer pays back the exact amount paid out by the bank.

At the same time as the customer enters into the diminishing ownership agreement he also enters into a lease agreement, whereby the bank agrees to lease its share of the house to the customer for a variable amount of rent. This lease agreement runs concurrent with the diminishing ownership agreement…

Both the amount repaid under the diminishing ownership agreement and the amount paid under the lease agreement are amalgamated and used to calculate how much of the bank's share of the property has been purchased per month by the customer. As the bank's share in the property decreases so does the amount paid under the lease agreement.

At the end of the twenty-five years, and if all the conditions contained within the two contracts have been met, the bank will pass title to the property to customer under the diminishing ownership agreement, normally for an additional payment.

NB - whilst some banks also require the customer to sign a third agreement under which the customer provides some form of security against payment of the amounts due under the other two contracts, other banks may also require more than three agreements to be signed.[194]

At the *Money Advice Service* website, DM is outlined as follows:

Diminishing Musharaka – also known as Musharakah – is essentially a co-ownership agreement. This means that both you and the bank or building society own the property together, with separate stakes. So each repayment – which is part rent and part capital (and part charges) – is used to purchase the bank's shares in the property over time. As your stake grows, the bank's stake shrinks. This reduces the amount of rent you then have to pay for use of the bank's share of the property.[195]

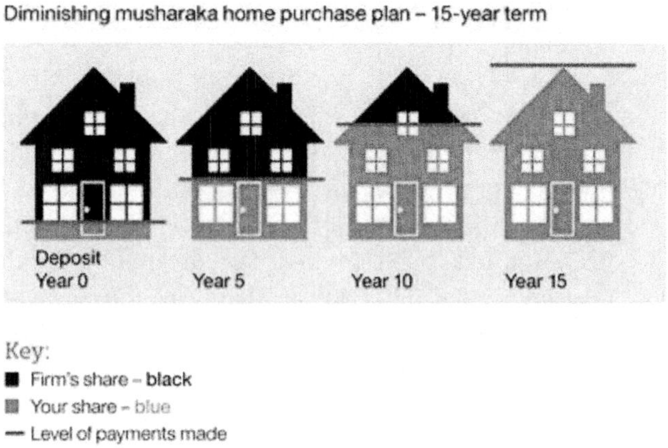

---

[194] http://www.hmrc.gov.uk/manuals/vatfinmanual/VATFIN8400.htm
[195] https://www.moneyadviceservice.org.uk

In summary, then the DM scheme involves the following steps:

Step 1: A (client) approaches B (Bank) to purchase *x*, a house.

Step 2: A and B enter into a *mushāraka* arrangement where A and B jointly agree to purchase the property. This is known in the traditional literature as *shirkat al-milk* ('partnership in property').[196]

Step 3: B owns 80% of the property and A owns 20%. B then leases his 80% share to A and charges rent to him for occupying the property proportionate to that share %. This is executed through what is called an *ijāra* ('leasing/renting') arrangement. This is a part rent and part capital aspect of the scheme.[197]

Step 4: A then promises to buy out the share % of B in units over an agreed term. The more % of B's share that A begins to purchase, the more the ownership % increases for A and diminishes or reduces for B. The rent that A pays to B while occupying the property is recalculated ('adjusted') to be proportionate with the remaining % share of B. The more B's ownership % declines, the less the rental payments are.

Step 5: the last share unit or % purchased by A from B transfers ownership or title deeds to A for an additional fee. A thus becomes complete owner of *x*.[198]

Thus, there are three major contracts in the MD scheme: partnership, lease and a promise. Some basic rules regarding this type of structured financing scheme include:

---

[196] al-Nabhānī, *The Economic System in Islam*, pp.136-147.
[197] Ibid., pp.77-104.
[198] Mufti Taqi Usmani, *An Introduction to Islamic Finance*, pp.57-64.

1. All contractual conditions outlined in Chapter Four apply here.

2. The different contracts in the various stages/steps of the scheme cannot be combined such that one is a condition for another because the Prophet forbade two contracts in one.

3. Each contract must be separate and drawn up with a valid offer and acceptance.

The Murābaḥa Housing Scheme (MHS/المرابحة):

The classical *Murābaḥa* contract was explained above and it is used as a house-financing scheme by many Islamic banks. Several explanations of it are given below:

> In Islamic financing structure, where an intermediary buys a property with free and clear title to it. The intermediary and prospective buyer then agree upon a sale price (including an agreed upon profit for the intermediary) that can be made through a series of instalments, or as a lump sum payment.
>
> Murabaha is not an interest-bearing loan, which is considered riba (or excess). Murabaha is an acceptable form of credit sale under Sharia (Islamic religious law). Similar in structure to a rent to own arrangement, the intermediary retains ownership of the property until the loan is paid in full.
>
> It is important to note that to prevent riba, the intermediary cannot be compensated in addition to the agreed upon terms of the contract. For this reason, if the buyer is late on their payments, the intermediary cannot charge any late penalties.[199]

---

[199] http://www.investopedia.com/terms/m/murabaha.asp

Another explanation has:

> Sale on profit. Technically a contract of sale in which the seller declares his cost and profit. This has been adopted as a mode of financing by a number of Islamic banks. As a financing technique, it involves a request by the client to the bank to purchase a certain item for him. The bank does that for a definite profit over the cost which is settled in advance. Some people have questioned the legality of this financing technique because of its similarity to *riba* or interest.
>
> Murabaha is the most popular and most common mode of Islamic financing. It is also known as Mark up or Cost plus financing. The word Murabaha is derived from the Arabic word Ribh that means profit. Originally, Murabaha was a contract of sale in which a commodity is sold on profit. The seller is obliged to tell the buyer his cost price and the profit he is making. This contract has been modified a little for application in the financial section its modern form Murabaha has become the single most popular technique of financing amongst the Islamic banks all over the world. It has been estimated that 80 to 90 percent of financial operations of some Islamic banks belong to this category. The Murabaha mode of finance operates in the following way: The client approaches an Islamic bank to get finance in order to purchase a specific commodity. An interest-based bank would lend the money on interest to this customer. The customer would go and buy the required commodity from the market. This option is not available to the Islamic bank, as it does not operate on the basis of interest. It cannot lend the money on interest. It cannot lend money with zero interest rate, as it has to make some money to stay in the business.
>
> Some portion of total finance may be offered as an interest free loan, however, the banking institutions have to make profit in order to stay in business.

> Hence, what course of action is open to the bank? The Murabaha model offers a solution. The bank purchases the commodity on cash and sells it to the customer on a profit. Since the client has no money, he buys the commodity on deferred payment basis. Thus, the client got the commodity for which he wanted the finance and the Islamic bank made some profit on the amount it had spent in acquiring the commodity.[200]

A further explanation:

> Murabahah is a particular kind of sale where the seller expressly mentions the cost of the sold commodity he has incurred, and sells it to another person by adding some profit or mark-up thereon.[201]
>
> The Bai' Murabahah involves purchase of a commodity by a bank on behalf of a client and its resale to the latter on cost-plus-profit basis. Under this arrangement the bank discloses its cost and profit margin to the client. In other words rather than advancing money to a borrower, which is how the system would work in a conventional banking agreement, the bank will buy the goods from a third party and sell those goods on to the customer for a pre-agreed price.[202]

In summary, then the MH scheme involves the following steps:

Step 1: Customer A approaches a bank B to purchase a property.

---

[200] http://www.islamic-banking.com/murabaha_sruling.aspx
[201] Mufti Taqi Usmani, *An Introduction to Islamic Finance*, p.71.
[202] http://sharia-banking.blogspot.co.uk/2006/10/al-murabaha.html

Step 2: A and B enter into a *Murābaḥa* contract where B will purchase the property and then will sell it to A with a disclosed % mark-up based on a pre-arranged agreement.

Step 3: A and B will then agree on a fixed term over which the price of the property will be paid (e.g. monthly for 20-25 years).

Step 4: upon receipt of the last payment, the property is transferred to ownership of A usually based on a fee.

Thus, the *modus operandi* of this contract is a sale followed by a sale with deferred payment. The basic rules of a MH scheme include:

1. The bank must have either actual or constructive possession (i.e. its control rights and liability) of the property before selling it to the customer.

2. The sale must be immediate and absolute without attributing it to a future date or making it conditional on a future contingent.

3. The mark-up or profit margin must be disclosed.

4. If the Bank appoints the client (customer) as its agent to purchase the property, then it cannot directly purchase the property from its customer as this would be a 'buy back' manoeuvre tantamount to *ribā*.

5. No penalty charge for defaulting on payments or changing the price of the arrangement because *Murābaḥa* is not a loan but a sale contract.

Ijāra Muntahiya bi ’l-Tamlīk (IMT/الإجارة منتهية بالتمليك):

A third home purchase plan offered by Islamic banks involves a renting contract that ultimately ends in purchase of the property. It is also known as *al-ijāra wa ’l-iqtinā` al-iājra thumma al-bay`*. It is explained as follows:

> ***Ijarah Muntahia-bi-tamleek*:** A lease ending in the transfer of the ownership to the lessee in such a way that the lease and sale are kept separate and independent transactions. Use of the this term for leasing is better known as *Ijarah wa iqtina*, as the latter tends to give the impression that the *Ijarah* and the sale are working side by side when actually they have to be two separate deals to fulfil the *Shari'ah* requirement.[203]
>
> ***Ijarah Mausufah bi Zimmah*** (a) An unidentified unit of asset is leased in the form of a forward lease. (b) A lease contract where the lessor undertakes to provide a well-defined service or benefit without identifying any particular of assets rendering the related service. Of a unit of the asset is destroyed, the contract is not terminated and the lessor provides another such unit.[204]
>
> ***Ijarah Wa Iqtina*** - Lease Agreement with option to acquire the leased asset at the end of the lease period. Often used in the context of home purchasing *Ijarah wa Iqtina* extends the concept of *Ijarah* to a hire and purchase agreement. It is a contract under which the Islamic bank finances equipment and machinery, building or other facilities for the customer against an agreed rental together with a unilateral undertaking by the bank or the customer that at the end of the lease period, the bank's ownership in the leased asset would be transferred to the customer. The rental is so fixed that the bank recovers its investment plus a profit.

---

[203] s.v. “Ijarah” available at http://www.islamic-banking.com/glossary.

[204] Ibid.

> *Ijarah wa Iqtina* extends the concept of *Ijarah* to a hire and purchase agreement. It is a contract under which the Islamic bank finances equipment and machinery, building or other facilities for the customer against an agreed rental together with a unilateral undertaking by the bank or the customer that at the end of the lease period, the bank's ownership in the leased asset would be transferred to the customer. The rental is so fixed that the bank recovers its investment plus a profit.[205]

Another explanation is:

> Also *ijarah muntahia bittamleek or ijarah thumma al-bai'*. By definition, it is an ijarah contract that ends up with the transfer of ownership of leased properties/assets from the lessor to the lessee at the end of the contract tenor. This type of *ijarah* (*ijarah* ended with ownership) may come in many forms, principal among which are: *ijarah muntahia bittamleek* that entails full transfer of ownership after the last installment has been paid, *ijarah muntahia bittamleek* that calls for full transfer of ownership after the end of the contract and for a preset price, and *ijarah muntahia bittamleek* which allows the lessee to choose from three options (purchase, renewal, termination) at the end of the lease tenor.[206]

Another explanation is:

> In Islamic Shariah, it is allowed that instead of sale, the lessor signs a separate promise to gift the leased asset to the lessee at the end of the lease period, subject to his payment of all amounts of rent. This arrangement is called *'Ijarah wa iqtina*. It has been allowed by a large number of

---

[205] Ibid.

[206] s.v. http://www.investment-and-finance.net/islamic-finance/i/ijarah-wa-iqtinaa.html with minor changes.

> contemporary scholars and is widely acted upon by the Islamic banks and financial institutions. The validity of this arrangement is subject to two basic conditions: a) The agreement of *Ijarah* itself should not be subjected to signing this promise of sale or gift but the promise should be recorded in a separate document. b) The promise should be unilateral and binding on the promisor only. It should not be a bilateral promise binding on both parties because in this case it will be a full contract effected to a future date, which is not allowed in the case of sale or gift.[207]

What is at the core in this kind of transaction then is a hire/rent contract followed by an option or promise to sell (sale contract). The basic steps to this mode of *ijāra* financing are:

Step 1: A (client/customer) approaches a Bank, B (financier) to purchase a property.

Step 2: B purchases a property for A and will sell it to A through deferred payment. At the same time, both enter into a lease agreement for a fixed term or period where A will make regular rental payments over that fixed period to B for use of B's asset. The rental payments also contribute towards amortization of the principal of the original property price.

Step 3: when the final rental payment is made by A to B, B will offer to sell the property to A for a pre-agreed price or gift it to A thus transferring full ownership to A based on an initial promise to do so.[208]

---

[207] See Mufti I. A. Usmani, *Meezan Bank's Guide to Islamic Financing*, pp.151-153 available at http://www.meezanbank.com

[208] See also Khan, *Islamic Economics and Finance*, p.85; Kettell, *Islamic Finance*, pp.55-65; Visser, *Islamic Finance*, pp.137-138; *Business Knowledge: IT in Islamic Finance*, pp.65-77 and Abdulkader, *Structuring Islamic Finance transactions*, pp.77-92.

The basic conditions of this kind of scheme include:

[1] Adherence to all conditions of a sale contract (outlined in chapter Five).

[2] The *ijāra* contract cannot be made conditional on the customer's promise to purchase the asset at the end of the rental period or fixed term. Both the *ijāra* contract and the sale contract must be kept separate.

[3] The promise made for the purchase of the property must be *unilateral* and not *bilateral* otherwise it would be tantamount to full affected to a future date which is not permitted for gifts or sales. The promise is binding only on the lessor (the Bank) and not the lessee (customer).

The Islamic viewpoint regarding Islamic Home Purchase Schemes:

The International Fiqh Academy Resolution No. 136 (15/2) 2004 and No. 110 (4/12) 2000 gave their verdict on DM and IMT schemes respectively:[209]

قرار رقم 136 (15/2)

بشأن المشاركة المتناقصة وضوابطها الشرعية

إن مجلس مجمع الفقه الإسلامي الدولي المنبثق عن منظمة المؤتمر الإسلامي المنعقد في دورته الخامسة عشرة بمسقط (سلطنة عُمان) **14 – 19** المحرم **1425**هـ، الموافق **6 – 11** آذار (مارس) **2004**م.

بعد اطلاعه على البحوث الواردة إلى المجمع بخصوص موضوع المشاركة المتناقصة وضوابطها الشرعية، وبعد استماعه إلى المناقشات التي دارت حوله،

---

[209] Texts taken from http://www.fiqhacademy.org.sa/qrarat/15-2.htm and http://www.fiqhacademy.org.sa/qrarat/12-4.htm respectively (= session 12, 1:313).

1. المشاركة المتناقصة: معاملة جديدة تتضمن شركة بين طرفين في مشروع ذي دخل، يتعهد فيها أحدهما بشراء حصة الطرف الآخر تدريجاً، سواء كان الشراء من حصة الطرف المشتري في الدخل، أم من موارد أخرى.

2. أساس قيام المشاركة المتناقصة: هو العقد الذي يبرمه الطرفان، ويسهم فيه كل منهما بحصة في رأس مال الشركة، سواء أكان إسهامه بالنقود أم بالأعيان، بعد أن يتم تقويمها، مع بيان كيفية توزيع الربح، على أن يتحمل كل منهما الخسارة – إن وجدت – بقدر حصته في الشركة.

3. تختص المشاركة المتناقصة بوجود وعد ملزم من أحد الطرفين فقط، بأن يتملك حصة الطرف الآخر، على أن يكون للطرف الآخر الخيار، وذلك بإبرام عقود بيع عند تملك كل جزء من الحصة، ولو بتبادل إشعارين بالإيجاب والقبول

4. يجوز لأحد أطراف المشاركة استئجار حصة شريكه بأجرة معلومة، ولمدة محددة، ويظل كل من الشريكين مسئولاً عن الصيانة الأساسية بمقدار حصته.

5. المشاركة المتناقصة مشروعة إذا التُزم فيها بالأحكام العامة للشركات، وروعيت فيها الضوابط الآتية:

أ – عدم التعهد بشراء أحد الطرفين حصة الطرف الآخر بمثل قيمة الحصة عند إنشاء الشركة، لما في ذلك من ضمان الشريك حصة شريكه، بل ينبغي أن يتم تحديد ثمن بيع الحصة بالقيمة السوقية يوم البيع، أو بما يتم الاتفاق عليه عند البيع.

ب – عدم اشتراط تحمّل أحد الطرفين مصروفات التأمين أو الصيانة وسائر المصروفات، بل تحمّل على وعاء المشاركة بقدر الحصص.

ج– تحديد أرباح أطراف المشاركة بنسب شائعة، ولا يجوز اشتراط مبلغ مقطوع من الأرباح أو نسبة من مبلغ المساهمة.

د- الفصل بين العقود والالتزامات المتعلقة بالمشاركة.

هـ- منع النص على حق أحد الطرفين في استرداد ما قدمه من مساهمة (تمويل)

قرار رقم: **110** (**12/4**)

بشأن موضوع

الإيجار المنتهي بالتمليك، وصكوك التأجير

إن مجلس مجمع الفقه الإسلامي الدولي المنبثق عن منظمة المؤتمر الإسلامي في دورته الثانية عشرة بالرياض في المملكة العربية السعودية، من **25** جمادى الآخرة **1421**هـ. **1** رجب **1421**هـ الموافق **23 – 28** أيلول (سبتمبر) **2000**م.

بعد اطلاعه على الأبحاث المقدمة إلى المجمع بخصوص موضوع (الإيجار المنتهي بالتمليك، وصكوك التأجير). وبعد استماعه إلى المناقشات التي دارت حول الموضوع بمشاركة أعضاء المجمع وخبرائه وعدد من الفقهاء.

قرر ما يلي:

الإيجار المنتهي بالتمليك:

أولا: ضابط الصور الجائزة والممنوعة ما يلي:

أ- ضابط المنع: أن يرد عقدان مختلفان، في وقت واحد، على عين واحدة، في زمن واحد.

ب- ضابط الجواز:

1. وجود عقدين منفصلين يستقل كل منهما عن الآخر، زمانا بحيث يكون إبرام عقد البيع بعد عقد الإجارة، أو وجود وعد بالتمليك في نهاية مدة الإجارة. والخيار يوازي الوعد في الأحكام.

2. أن تكون الإجارة فعلية وليست ساترة للبيع.

ج- أن يكون ضمان العين المؤجرة على المالك لا على المستأجر وبذلك يتحمل المؤجر ما يلحق العين من غير تلف ناشئ من تعدي المستأجر أو تفريطه، ولا يلزم المستأجر بشيء إذا فاتت المنفعة.

إذا اشتمل العقد على تأمين العين المؤجرة فيجب أن يكون التأمين تعاونيا إسلاميا لا تجاريا ويتحمله المالك المؤجر وليس المستأجر.

د- يجب أن تطبق على عقد الإجارة المنتهية بالتمليك أحكام الإجارة طوال مدة الإجارة وأحكام البيع عند تملك العين.

هـ- تكون نفقات الصيانة غير التشغيلية على المؤجر لا على المستأجر طوال مدة الإجارة.

ثانيا: من صور العقد الممنوعة:

أ- عقد إجارة ينتهي بتملك العين المؤجرة مقابل ما دفعه المستأجر من أجرة خلال المدة المحددة، دون إبرام عقد جديد، بحيث تنقلب الإجارة في نهاية المدة بيعا تلقائياً.

ب- إجارة عين لشخص بأجرة معلومة، ولمدة معلومة، مع عقد بيع له معلق على سداد جميع الأجرة المتفق عليها خلال المدة المعلومة، أو مضاف إلى وقت في المستقبل.

ج- عقد إجارة حقيقي واقترن به بيع بخيار الشرط لصالح المؤجر، ويكون مؤجلا إلى أجل طويل محدد (هو آخر مدة عقد الإيجار).

د– وهذا ما تضمنته الفتاوى والقرارات الصادرة من هيئات علمية، ومنها هيئة كبار العلماء بالمملكة العربية السعودية.

ثالثا: من صور العقد الجائزة:

أ– عقد إجارة يُمكّن المستأجر من الانتفاع بالعين المؤجرة، مقابل أجرة معلومة في مدة معلومة، واقترن به عقد هبة العين للمستأجر، معلقا على سداد كامل الأجرة وذلك بعقد مستقل، أو وعد بالهبة بعد سداد كامل الأجرة، وذلك وفق ما جاء في قرار المجمع بالنسبة للهبة رقم **13**(**3/1**).

ب– عقد إجارة مع إعطاء المالك الخيار للمستأجر بعد الانتهاء من وفاء جميع الأقساط الإيجارية المستحقة خلال المدة في شراء العين المأجورة بسعر السوق عند انتهاء مدة الإجارة، وذلك وفق قرار المجمع رقم **44**(**5/6**).

ج– عقد إجارة يمكّن المستأجر من الانتفاع بالعين المؤجرة، مقابل أجرة معلومة في مدة معلومة، واقترن به وعد ببيع العين المؤجرة للمستأجر بعد سداد كامل الأجرة بثمن يتفق عليه الطرفان.

د– عقد إجارة يمكّن المستأجر من الانتفاع بالعين المؤجرة، مقابل أجرة معلومة، في مدة معلومة، ويعطي المؤجر للمستأجر حق الخيار في تملك العين المؤجرة في أي وقت يشاء، على أن يتم البيع في وقته بعقد جديد بسعر السوق، وذلك وفق قرار المجمع السابق رقم **44**(**5/6**)، أو حسب الاتفاق في وقته.

رابعا: هناك صور من عقود التأجير المنتهي بالتمليك محل خلاف وتحتاج إلى دراسة تعرض في دورة قادمة إن شاء الله تعالى.

صكوك التأجير:

قرر المجمع تأجيل موضوع صكوك التأجير لمزيد من البحث والدراسة ليطرح في دورة لاحقة.

A number of objections have been raised against these home finance schemes offered by Islamic Banks or retail banks with a structured Shariah-compliant product portfolio. Some of these objections (included in the Fiqh Academy Resolutions above) are:

[1] Disguised *ribā*: Often, sceptics of Islamic home finance schemes see these contracts as essentially a 'paying money to get more money', tactic, i.e. the asset being exchanged acts merely as a prop while money is in effect exchanged (loaned) for more money in return. Another criticism is that in the DM scheme, for example, the banks guarantees profit for itself, which contravenes the rulings of partnership contracts that requires linking reward with risk because if risk is eliminated, the reward resembles interest.

[2] *Gharar*: Some of the home purchase schemes have elements of *gharar*. For example, in the DM and IMT schemes, it is not clear whether the customer is a tenant or a buyer or both. The problem is that intolerable uncertainty is sufficient to invalidate a contract in Shariah. Another example is that the rental rate or rent level for these schemes is set against the LIBOR (London Interbank Offered Rate), which is an estimated interest rate set by banks for internal lending activity; it goes up and down and is never fixed. Setting rental rates according to the LIBOR benchmark generates *gharar* and *jahāla* in the tenant's rental amount. They will not know exactly what amount they will be paying because the rent will always be adjusted with the change in the LIBOR. With a customer bound to a long-term rental contract, adjustments in rental rates may make payments beyond affordability in cases of dramatic increases in the LIBOR.

[3] Replicating conventional mortgages: Some scholars argue that the economics in the Islamic home financing schemes replicate conventional mortgages. Hence, in form and real terms, there is no difference at all.

[4] Combining Contracts: Some scholars see the housing finance schemes offered by Islamic banks or retail banks with Islamic personal finance products as normalising combination of contracts, i.e. making them overlap or depend on each other even though they appear to be discrete in the entire scheme. For example, in the *Murābaḥa* scheme, the banks usually require a declaration of purchase or promise to purchase from the customer if the bank acquires the property for him. Banks will not purchase the property for the customer if no such declaration or promise is first secured. In this way, the bank is actually guaranteeing for itself money by obviating any meaningful ownership of the property because it sells the property to the customer with the profit mark-up based on this promise virtually without delay.

[5] Client bears loss: In *Murābaḥa* and *Mushāraka* schemes that involve rental payments, often the client or customer bears the risk of any loss, depreciation or fall in price of the property. This contravenes the basic conditions of *ijāra* where the tenant or lessee is not owner of the property but owner of the usufruct. Thus, it is not clear why any risk in the fall in the value of the property is compensated by the tenant who is not the owner. Yet, Islamic banks stipulate the condition that the client compensates for the fall in capital value of the property.

[6] Deferred counter-values: Another criticism of Islamic home finance schemes is how they involve no immediate exchange of either of the counter-values (price and property) – which is a condition of a sale contract – because both are deferred to a later date, i.e. the customer will acquire the property once the last rental payment is made and the bank will pass the title deeds when that is fulfilled for a disclosed fee.

Therefore, in light of the above outlines on the basic objections raised against Islamic home purchase plans, it appears that these schemes contain discrete contracts that are valid in themselves, but taken as whole produce a complexity that problematizes its overall soundness. Nevertheless, despite these objections, Muslim scholars and Shariah finance specialist continue to disagree on the permissibility of such schemes and the disagreement is no doubt likely to continue.

Islamic Finance: *General Challenges*

Some general problems related to prevalent Shariah-Complaint personal finance services and products include:

[1] Convoluted Contracts: Often, Shariah-compliant financial transactions involve several layers of transactions with meticulous conditions that are not permitted to be combined or overlapped. This in the end proves cumbersome, tedious as well as complicated and in many cases adds additional costs for Islamic financiers that are subsequently passed on to the customers.

[2] Not-profitable: Many argue that Islamic financial products, whether for personal finance or other, is simply not profitable for banks or financial institutions hence there has been a large downsizing of Islamic finance departments and expertise (cf. HSBC Amanah finance closure).

[3] Weakly Islamic: It is argued that the Shariah principles of commercial transaction are only followed in 'form' but not 'substance' by Islamic banks. In other words, Islamic contracts are adhered to in its legal and technical aspect – i.e. on paper – rather than in the particulars of those contracts. Thus, contracts do not exactly represent the details of the finance operations and schemes.

[4] Wide-ranging: Because there is no official auditing body that regulates and assesses Shariah-compliant products (and due to the legal differences within legal Schools [*madhhabs*]), there is difference over what constitutes sound Islamic financial transactions to be converted into modes of finance.

[5] Excessive Cost: Often, due to the convoluted and complex series of transactions underpinning the transference of asset ownership to clients/customers, Islamic finance contracts incur cost and additional taxes, which are passed on to customers. This is considerably unattractive for anyone looking to secure a good deal on their personal finance plans.

Concluding Remarks

Although Shariah-compliant finance products are forecast for huge growth over the next decade – indicative of their demand and profitability – nevertheless, it is important to bear in mind that the contracts that these products are based on are not in origin finance contracts but sale contracts. They have been engineered as modes of finance. For this reason, it is inevitable that in some aspects these contracts will service a need and offer financial productivity whereas in other aspects they will be artificial and convoluted with all the limitations and contraventions of Shariah contract regulations discussed in the previous chapters.

It is also to be remembered that Shariah-compliant products are not ends in themselves but temporary means for an alternative finance package. Hence, the aim through these structured products is not to substitute or replace transactions that naturally operate within an Islamic economic system but to service an immediate need for consumption of Shariah-defined products. Therefore, Shariah-compliant finance must not be seen as replacing full implementation of the Islamic economic system that is integrated into the collective systems of Islam that constitute the Khilāfah. Only under the Khilāfah, authentic realisation of Islam's economic principles is possible.

Key References

In addition to the website references and various books cited in the chapters, key English references for Islamic contracts and finance in general are listed below.

Ayub, M. *Understanding Islamic Finance*, Sussex: John Wiley and Sons, 2007.

Elkhatib, D. A. *The ABA Practical Guide to Drafting Basic Islamic Finance Contracts*, U.S.A.: ABA Association, 2013.

Hassan, A. *Sales and Contracts in Early Islam*, Delhi: Kitab Bhavan, 1997.

Iqbal, Z. and Mirakhor, A. *An Introduction to Islamic Finance*, Singapore: John Wiley and Sons, 2007.

Jamaldeen, F. *Islamic Finance for Dummies*, N.J.: John Wiley and Sons, 2012.

Kettell, B. *Islamic Finance in a Nutshell*, Sussex: John Wiley and Sons, 2010.

Mansuri, M. T. *Islamic Law of Contracts and business Transactions*, Delhi: Adam Publishers and Distributors, 2006.

Qfinance, *Islamic Finance: Instruments and Markets*, London: Bloomsbury Information Ltd, 2010.

Saleem, M. Y. *Islamic Commercial Law*, Singapore: John Wiley and Sons, 2013.

Usmani, T. *An Introduction to Islamic Finance*,

al-Zuḥaylī, W. *Financial Transactions in Islamic Jurisprudence*, trans. M. al-Gamal, 2 vols. Dār El-Fikr, 2003.

~Notes~

Short Financial Glossary

Based on http://www.islamic-banking.com with minor adjustments and editing. For other definitions of Islamic financial terms, refer to the relevant chapters they occur in.

`Aqd العقد: Contract, Agreement, Bond. It is synonymous with the word 'contract' in modern law.

`Arbūn الأربون: A non-refundable down payment or deposit paid by a buyer for the right to purchase goods at a certain time and certain price in future; if the right is exercised, it becomes part of the purchase price. If the buyer does not complete the purchase or withdraws for any reason, the seller has the option to forfeit the deposit. Also known as *`Urbūn* and *Bay` al-`Arbūn*.

**`Ayn** العين: Monetary wealth. A tangible (physical) asset; also, refers to currency or ready money. *`Ayn* is often contrasted with *dayn* (see s.v.).

Bay` البيع: Stands for 'sale' or contract of sale. It is often used as a prefix in referring to different sales-based modes of Islamic finance.

Collateral Assets pledged to secure the repayment of a loan.

Ḍamān الضمان: Guarantee, liability.

Ḍarūra الضرورة: Necessity, overriding necessity. Adopting a ruling, even one that may contravene a Shariah rule, when one is compelled by extreme necessity, usually life or death (Usually used for the "Doctrine of Necessity," whereby something otherwise prohibited becomes temporarily permissible).

Dayn — الدين: Debt. A *dayn* comes into existence as the result of any contract or credit transaction.

Faḍl — الفضل: Excess, addition, excess, gain or surplus.

Gharar — الغرر: Lit: uncertainty, hazard, chance or risk; denotes deception or an exchange in which one or both parties stand to be deceived through ignorance of an essential element of exchange; also refers to intolerable contractual ambiguity.

Ijāra — الإجارة: Lit. letting or lease. Technically, sale of a definite usufruct in exchange for a definite reward. Commonly used for wages, it also refers to a contract of land lease at a fixed rent payable in cash.

Jahāla — الجهالة: Lack of knowledge, ignorance. In contracts, it refers to lack of information on the subject, or ambiguity in the terms and conditions of the contract; also refers to uncertainty, conjecture and an unspecified element in the quality, quantity or price of goods.

Khiyār — الخيار: Lit. option, choice. The option to rescind or cancel a sales contract in certain conditions, for example a defect in the goods.

Mushāraka — المشاركة: The literal meaning of *Mushāraka* is sharing, an investment partnership with profit-loss-sharing implications; also a contract of partnership in which two or more partners provide capital and share profits or losses as the case may be; an investment partnership with profit-and-loss sharing.

Mu`āmalāt — المعاملات: Dealings between humans. Lit. economic transactions related to exchange of goods and services. Also includes financial transaction.

Principal — In commercial law, the principal is the amount that is received, in the case of a loan, or the amount from which accrues the interest.

Qarḍ — القرض: Loan. Lit: to cut or cut off. It is so called because the property (in terms of wealth) of a person (the lender) is cut off and transferred to a needy person (the borrower) without expecting any return or profit. The borrower is required to repay only the principal amount to the lender on demand.

Qarḍ Ḥasan — قرض حسن: A virtuous loan. Loan in the meaning of a virtuous loan that is interest-free and extended on a goodwill basis, mainly for welfare purpose; the borrower is only required to pay back the borrowed amount. The loan is payable on demand and repayment is obligatory. However, if a debtor is in difficulty, the lender/creditor is expected to extend time or even to voluntarily waive repayment of the whole or a part of the loan amount. Islam allows loan as a form of social service among the rich to help the poor and those who are in need of financial assistance.

Qimār — القمار: Lit. gambling. Technically an agreement in which possession of a property is contingent upon the occurrence of an uncertain event. By implication it applies to those agreements in which there is a definite loss for one party and definite gain for the other without specifying which party will gain and which party will lose. Another word for gambling is *Maysir*.

Ribā — الربا: Lit. increase or addition. Technically, it denotes any increase or addition to capital obtained by the lender as a condition of the loan. In simple terms *ribā* covers any return on money on money, whether the interest rate is fixed, floating, simple or compounded and at whatever rate which is guaranteed irrespective of the performance of the investment, is considered *ribā* and is so prohibited.

Salaf — السلف: In a wider sense, it refers to a loan which draws forth no profit for the creditor and is slightly different from *qarḍ* in that an amount given as *salaf* cannot be called back before it is due; it includes loans for specified periods, i.e. short, intermediate and long-term loans.

Ṣarf — الصرف: Currency exchange. In pre-Islamic times it was exchange of gold for gold, silver for silver and gold for silver or vice versa. In Islamic jurisprudence such exchange is regarded as 'sale of price for price' (*bay` al thaman bi 'l-thaman*), and each price is consideration of the other. It also means sale of monetary value for monetary value in currency exchange, such as buying and selling of currencies.

Shariah-Compliant — Term used in Islamic finance to denote a financial product or activity that complies with the requirements of the Shariah, e.g. 'Shariah compliant financing' or 'Shariah compliant investment'. Islamic finance derives its principles from the Shariah, which is based on the Qur'an and the *Sunna* of the Prophet Muhammad.

Wa`d — الوعد: Promise, undertaking. A promise, such

as is found in purchase and sale undertakings used in certain Islamic finance transactions; a promise to buy or sell certain goods in a certain quantity at a certain time in future at a certain price.

Printed in Great Britain
by Amazon

82883030R00108